Themes from the Gospel of John

Themes from the Gospel of John

Michael Hickey

HAMILTON BOOKS
AN IMPRINT OF
ROWMAN & LITTLEFIELD
Lanham • Boulder • New York • London

Published by Hamilton Books
An imprint of The Rowman & Littlefield Publishing Group, Inc.
4501 Forbes Boulevard, Suite 200, Lanham, Maryland 20706
www.rowman.com

6 Tinworth Street, London SE11 5AL, United Kingdom

Copyright © 2021 by The Rowman & Littlefield Publishing Group, Inc.

All rights reserved. No part of this book may be reproduced in any form or by any electronic or mechanical means, including information storage and retrieval systems, without written permission from the publisher, except by a reviewer who may quote passages in a review.

British Library Cataloguing in Publication Information Available

Library of Congress Control Number: 2021932677
ISBN 978-0-7618-7270-2 (pbk.)
ISBN 978-0-7618-7271-9 (electronic)

In many ways, the seeds of this book were scattered by the Holy Spirit who used my faculty advisor, the late Fr. Dan Harrington, S.J., at Weston/Boston College School of Theology and Ministry to cultivate those seeds and re-plant them in rows of themes. Fr. Harrington had been the Chair of Biblical Studies at the college and served as the Editor of New Testament Abstracts in the United States. In addition to being my faculty advisor, I also considered Fr. Dan to be my good friend and spiritual father. I dedicate this book to his fond memory.

* * *

I would also like to thank Brother Michael O'Neill McGrath, OSFS for granting his permission to use his imaginative artwork depicting John the Evangelist for the cover of this book.

Contents

Chapter 1: Themes   1

Chapter 2: Background   5

PART I: THE FOUR MAJOR THEMES

Chapter 3: The Logos (Jn. Chapter 1)   17

Chapter 4: The Book of Signs (Jn. Chapters 2–12)   29

Chapter 5: The Book of Glory (Jn. Chapters 13–20)   47

Chapter 6: The Epilogue (Jn. Chapter 21)   55

PART II: THE SUB-THEMES

Chapter 7: The "I AM" Sayings   63

Chapter 8: Faith and Believing   69

Chapter 9: Knowing and Unknowing   75

Chapter 10: Light and Darkness   81

Chapter 11: Seeing and Blindness   87

Chapter 12: Ascent and Descent   93

Chapter 13: Life and Death   99

Chapter 14: Abiding and Discipleship   107

Chapter 15: Bread and Water ... 113
Chapter 16: Love ... 123
Chapter 17: Two Extended Allegories ... 137
Chapter 18: Judgment and The World ... 145
Chapter 19: Son of Man-Son of God ... 157
Chapter 20: Spirit, Paraclete and Truth ... 165

Index ... 171
About the Author ... 177

Chapter 1

Themes

What is a Theme?

A theme is a thoughtful idea, concept or belief that intentionally recurs and creatively pervades a work of literature. It is part of an underlying central message which is universal in its nature. A theme not only applies to specific characters or events but expresses a broader truth applicable to human experience. Any story can contain several themes, however, each one in its significance, should unify what the author is attempting to convey. A theme should be able to be stated most often in just one word or in just a few words and need not be stated explicitly, but implied and expressed through a character's words and deeds or actions. They should cause the reader to think about and reflect on the underlying message and how it gives a deeper meaning to the story. Themes should guide the reader to a more complete grasp of the entire story by facilitating an intimate connection between the reader and that particular story. It can connect several essential elements of the overall story such as characters, plot, conflicts, and resolution, interactions, settings, and events. The theme threads the narrative into a single and complete piece of work.

Many stories contain both themes and sub-themes. They are similar in that they both connect with the underlying message of the story; however sub-themes are different in that they are specific and subordinate themes within the broader context of the major theme or themes. They are not disorganized as much as being unorganized and diffused throughout the story. This does not render them any less important in their connection to the message which the author is intending to convey. Themes are not always obvious and often you won't notice them unless you look for them. On the other hand, you would surely miss them if they weren't there. The overall story would seem like a lifeless body without any blood and bones to hold it together. Themes are far more abstract than concrete. Therefore, because they are often so elusive and sometimes found hiding in support of the overall story, they do not lend themselves as much to being taught as they do to being caught.

THEMES AND SUB-THEMES IN THE GOSPEL OF JOHN

The Gospel of John leans itself nicely toward trying to understand it and its message as a complete Gospel through its themes. It is a story about the divine person of Jesus Christ who came from above, entered history and became a human being. Its four themes and many sub-themes are vibrant and bring the underlying message of the story to life in a way that simply reading the words of this gospel from beginning to end might not. The main character or hero is the *Logos,* the Word of God, who is Jesus Christ, and the *Logos* Prologue is the first of the four major themes in this Gospel. It is the *Logos* prologue (Chapter 1), which sets the stage for all other themes and is perhaps the key theme. It is the intention of Jesus, the *Logos* to bring to us the Kingdom of God/Eternal Life, which is within him, and can then be described consequently, as being "in our midst."

Following the *Logos* theme, The Book of Signs (Chapters 2-12) is a second major theme consisting of a series of seven events which are signs and miracles, such as the wedding at Cana, the healings of the royal official's son, the paralytic, and the blind man, followed by the feeding of the five thousand, as well as the walking on water, and the raising of Lazarus. Through this second major theme, the Evangelist John will show us through his words and deeds how Jesus is the long-awaited Messiah. This theme is designed by John with a series of seven signs or miracles to ultimately bring us to faith and belief in Jesus Christ as the Son of God. The twist in the story, however, will be that Jesus will not be the kind of Messiah the nation of Israel had been expecting throughout their recorded history.

Because the story's central character and hero Jesus, the *Logos*, will be in serious conflict with several of the scholars of the law and the religious officials, this will lead to a third major theme called the Book of Glory (Chapters 13-20). Here in this third major theme, this conflict will bring about Jesus' glorification through his death on the cross and ultimately lead to his resurrection from the dead and His ascension. The fourth and last major theme will be the final chapter which is called the Epilogue (Chapter 21), which is seen as a later addition, possibly added at another point in time by John the Evangelist himself, but more probably added later by a disciple of John.

Throughout this entire Gospel story, John will thread several sub-themes that are not placed in any continuous chapters like the major themes, but will weave in and out of all four major themes, strengthening the underlying message of the story. The sub-themes that are not in separate sections of this Gospel like the major themes but interspersed throughout are: The "I AM" sayings, Faith and Believing, Knowing and Unknowing, Light and Darkness, Seeing and Blindness, Ascent and Descent, Life and Death, The Two Extended Allegories, Judgment and the World, Son of Man-Son of God, Love, Abiding and Discipleship, Bread and Water, and Spirit-Paraclete and Truth. These sub-themes are certainly no less important than the major themes in conveying the story's central message. These sub-themes and major themes are critical to understanding why the Gospel of John is often described as the most spiritual of the four canonical Gospels. Unlike the synoptic Gospels of Matthew, Mark, and Luke this Gospel story's emphasis is on the Divine Jesus who came from the heavenly world above and became a human being. For that reason, its symbol is an eagle in flight which soars into the farthest reaches of the sky and then descends to earth. Like the spirit, the four major themes and the several sub-themes of this story will be the threads that weave it all together and enable it to become like a finished piece of fine embroidered tapestry.

It appears that the Gospel writer John was most intentional in his insertion of the major themes which separate the Gospel into four continuous sections, as well as the many sub-themes that he interspersed throughout the entire story. John wrote his Gospel story in a manner which would allow us to better uncover the many themes, then see and understand the underlying and deeper spiritual message he wanted to convey. Furthermore, it would allow us to connect with his Gospel and with Jesus through the Holy Spirit in ways that the synoptic Gospels of Matthew, Mark, and Luke could not allow. The synoptic Gospel writers begin their stories with Jesus' human birth, origins and baptism and piece their narratives together with intentional similarity and in harmony with each other. Whereas fully ninety percent of the material in John's Gospel is different, beginning with its starting point in the heavenly world above. Additionally, the synoptics are more descriptive in their approach and John is more reflective in his. The apostles could not understand fully who Jesus was at the time they observed him and therefore could not fully understand the events that were occurring before their very eyes even though they did record them. John is writing his Gospel much later than the synoptic writers and his Gospel is written moreover from a post-resurrection point of view. John writes as he reflects on the events and tries to understand their significance. He then attempts to communicate with us through his several themes which have much richness, symbolism, and often multiple meanings.

There is little mention of the Kingdom of God in John and far more emphasis on what he calls, "Eternal Life," which John sees as occurring in the now moment; as eternity happening essentially in the present time. His Gospel will envision Jesus more as coming from above to save us in the eternal now rather than being ahead later at the second coming to bring the Kingdom of God in its fullness. The themes are reflectively designed by him to help us see and discover his Gospel's "realized eschatology"[1] or realized end times, i.e., the last things in the now moment. The synoptic Gospel writers did not take a focused thematic approach to their story. This does not render the other three Gospels as being any less powerful than the Gospel of John, only different in their approach to the Gospel message. The synoptic Gospels convey a no less profound but very concrete message, whereas because of its many themes, John's Gospel is far more abstract and multivariant. This makes grasping John's underlying message through his themes akin to playing that old children's game of "Hide and Seek." Finally, as St Augustine said long ago concerning this Gospel: "The Gospel of John is like a body of water which is shallow enough for little children to wade in, yet so deep that elephants can swim in it." [2]

NOTES

1. "Realized Eschatology," Brown, Raymond, SJ, ed., Jerome Biblical Commentary, (Englewood Cliffs, NJ, Prentice-Hall Publishing, 1968), Sec. 78:89–90; 80:46–47.
2. "Augustine," The Internet Encyclopedia of Philosophy, ISSN 2161-0002, https://www.iep.utm.edu/, Nov. 28, 2020, https://www.augustinus.it/links/inglese/opere.htm

Chapter 2

Background

John, the writer of this Gospel, is also considered as the author of the Johannine Epistles and the Book of Revelation/The Apocalypse, the last book of the Bible. He was one of the twelve Apostles of Jesus and as an apostle became an eyewitness to much of what Jesus said and did. He was an eyewitness to the many signs or miracles of Jesus. He was also an eyewitness to Jesus' glorification through the cross, resurrection, and ascension. As you might remember, John was very close to Jesus. In fact, he was called "the disciple whom Jesus loved" as well as "the Beloved Disciple."

    John was the son of Zebedee and the brother of the Apostle James. In his later years, Polycarp who became Bishop of Smyrna and Irenaeus, Bishop of Lyon became disciples of John. The church Father Ignatius, Bishop of Antioch was also a disciple of his. John is said to have been the only apostle who died of natural causes as an old man. All the other apostles were brutally tortured and martyred in different ways. He is said to have died in Ephesus in a home he had lived in with Mary, the mother of Jesus, who was given to him as his mother at the cross of Christ and traditionally given to us as our mother as well. Today, there is a home in Ephesus that was pointed out to my wife Terri and I while we were on a tour of Greece and Turkey in 2016 which tradition says is that particular home. Who really knows for sure? It could be factual; it could also be simply folklore. A few of the more famous works of art depicting the Apostle John have been painted by Pieter Paul Rubens and El Greco. Both paintings are part of the Prado Collection. My wife and I viewed them both on a visit to the Prado Museum in Madrid, during a tour of Spain in 1999.

    Enough about John and any of the fine details concerning tradition, folklore or Johannine art for now, let's get more into the background to the Gospel he wrote. The Hebrew Tradition historically began with a genealogy. If you will recall, the synoptic Gospels of Matthew, Mark, and Luke all contain some form of genealogy of Jesus. But unlike the human genealogy accounted for in those other three canonical Gospels, John's genealogical account is of Jesus Christ's pre-existent divine origins and not his human origins. John takes us "behind the scenes," and allows us to see the eternal origin and divine nature of Jesus. He will tell us how as the *Logos*, the Word of God, Jesus was present with God, the Father at creation, God in action, creating, then revealing and becoming human as God revealed, for our redemption and salvation.

In terms of dating, this Gospel could have appeared in written form as early as 70–80 AD or as late as 90–100 AD; the latter dating is more probable and most Biblical scholars fix the date at about the year 90 AD. It is further believed that it may have been circulating in an oral tradition much earlier than that. It is likely that John wrote his Gospel in Ephesus which is in Asia Minor and is now located in modern day Turkey. That is the locus according to Ignatius of Antioch, a disciple of John who wrote shortly after John, to the early Christian community. Toward the Gospel's end, John will tell us the primary reasons for his writing it as an authentic testimony to Jesus: "written that men might believe that Jesus is the Christ, the Son of God and thus have life in his name (Jn. 20:31)." [12]

WHAT MAKES JOHN'S GOSPEL DIFFERENT?

In John, as was stated earlier, unlike the synoptic Gospels of Matthew, Mark, and Luke, there is no earthly birth and genealogy. That is only one difference, there are many more. Here are some of the other differences between the synoptic Gospels and the Gospel of John:

1. In John, there are no parables, just a few extended allegories (such as The Good Shepherd [Ch. 10] and The True Vine [Ch. 15]).
2. In John, there are no exorcisms.
3. In John, there aren't as many miracles, but there are seven signs in the Book of Signs, also no Book of Glory in the synoptics as there is in John.
4. Synoptics have one visit to Jerusalem, In John there are many.
5. Last Supper account is the Passover meal in the synoptics and the Last Supper is before the Passover meal in John.
6. Unlike synoptics "Love Your neighbors/Love Your Enemies," John says: "Love One Another."
7. In synoptics, Peter is most prominent Apostle; In John, it is the Beloved Disciple, Mary Magdalene, Martha of Bethany.
8. In the synoptics, the Kingdom of God is coming; it is ahead. In John, there is not too much mention of the Kingdom; there is more focus on Eternal Life which begins now; it is not ahead; it is above.

9. In John, there is no Sermon on the Mount, Beatitudes, or Lord's Prayer, no ethical teachings, no Transfiguration story, all of which are in the synoptics.
10. In John, there is no prediction of Jesus return. Jesus is eternally present.
11. No Ascension narrative in John.
12. In John, Women play a much more prominent role.
13. Also, not in synoptics and only in John, is the *Logos* Prologue account, Book of Signs beginning with Cana wedding, dialogue with Nicodemus, washing of the feet, woman at the well story, Lazarus raised account, the Paraclete account, the True Vine allegory, the woman caught in adultery, the resurrection appearance to Mary Magdalene and then another appearance to Thomas.
14. In John, there are several harsh statements against the Jews.
15. There are two endings (Epilogues) to the Gospel of John. This is not the case in the synoptics.
16. In the synoptics, the Gospel story is seen as Christology from below; In John, it is seen as Christology from above or High Christology vs Low Christology.

There are numerous other minor differences as well.

Although it seems John was familiar with the synoptics, especially Mark which was really the first Gospel (not Matthew as in the canon), he made no effort to harmonize or synchronize with them as they purposefully did with each other. Matthew, Mark, and Luke are called synoptic Gospels because they parallel each other and they are similar in content, order, and statements. It seems that John set out to write an entirely different Gospel from an entirely different perspective, focusing on the divine origins of the earthly Jesus. Why? First, John's context and setting was entirely different. It was believed that he more than likely wrote this Gospel in Ephesus, but it is also remotely possible that John wrote it on the Greek island of Patmos where he was imprisoned in exile. Patmos, at the time, was a Roman penal colony. John's brother James the Apostle was supposedly martyred on Patmos. Its more certain that John wrote the Book of Revelation/The Apocalypse on Patmos; we are surer of that. On the other hand, it appears that his Gospel was more likely written in Ephesus across the sea from Patmos. The basis for that belief we receive from some of the writings of the Church Fathers.

Back in the year 2016, my wife, Terri and I visited Ephesus in modern day Turkey where John supposedly wrote his Gospel and then the cave at Patmos in Greece where John along with one of his disciples continued to write as an old man. The cave now rests beneath the bottommost part of a Greek Orthodox church on Patmos which is St John the Evangelist church. It was a very spiritual experience for us to descend the many steps beneath the church to the cave. Amazingly, the cave is very well preserved since the time John was there as an old man. We saw the solid rock altar he is said to have prayed at, the hard rocks he slept on as his pillows. It was an especially thrilling spiritual experience for me to look out the rock hewn window to see the view of the same harbor he looked at from that window back in the early centuries of the Christian church. Supposedly, it was in this cave on Patmos that John had a vision of Jesus which he later recorded in the Book of Revelation as he was listening for God's voice and heard the Lord say: "I Am the Alpha and the Omega, the one who is and who was and who is to come, the Almighty (Rv. 1:8)."

If we believe truly that sacred scripture is the Word of God, in order for us to hear God's voice today, as John did then, requires first our listening and then our hearing. There is a difference. When the Lord called Samuel the prophet as a young boy, he was instructed to respond: "Speak, Lord, your servant is listening (1 Sm. 3:9)."

As modern Catholic scripture scholar Mary Healey has pointed out: "Today, we must admit to ourselves that our prayers to the Lord often sound more like: 'Listen, Lord, your servant is speaking.'" [3]

Now, let's look at some more of the differences between John's Gospel and the synoptic Gospels. How do we account for the many differences? The likely answer is that John was writing in a different context and at a different time than the synoptics as it was probably very close to the end of the first century. John is addressing the many issues of importance and concern for the church of his day. The synoptic Gospels were written much earlier than John's Gospel, probably from 50 to 70 AD. At the time they were written, the key issue for the synoptics to address for the new Christian church was to show that Jesus was the long-awaited Jewish Messiah and the fulfillment of all the Old Testament prophecies and promises. They showed how the Kingdom of God, somewhere between already and not yet, had arrived in Jesus. Those Gospels would address how the Kingdom of God came in a different way than was expected and how Jesus, as the crucified Messiah, was vindicated and confirmed through his resurrection and exaltation—how he had been truly lifted-up and now sits at the right hand of God. John is writing somewhat later when the church was confronting some different challenges, particularly the spread of much heresy. His writing was also more greatly influenced by the spread of Hellenism throughout the world at that time.

THE RISE OF HERESY

One of the challenges John was facing at the time he wrote his Gospel was the reality that false teachers and many heretics had arisen in the church. At this time, many are questioning and challenging the deity of Christ. Many are claiming that Jesus is not fully God. On the other hand, some are also questioning his true humanity, and they are denying that God Almighty would ever become a human being. So, John from the get-go, from his opening lines in his *Logos* prologue will confirm both the full divinity and the true humanity of Jesus. He will tell us of Jesus' divine pre-existence and then subsequently about his full humanity even in his opening verses beginning in verse 1 of Chapter 1:

> In the beginning was the Word (*The Logos*, Gk.), and the Word (*The Logos*, Gk.) was with God, and the Word (*The Logos*, Gk.) was God. He was in the beginning with God (Jn. 1:1-2).

Then in verse 14 of the same opening chapter: "And the Word (the *Logos*, Gk.) became flesh and made his dwelling among us, and we saw his glory, the glory as of the Father's only Son, full of grace and truth (Jn. 1:14)."

From the beginning of his gospel, John will set out to silence the naysayers, primarily those questioning Jesus' divinity, but also some who were questioning his humanity as well.

Many of the first heresies which arose in the church which the Evangelist John was addressing through the writing of his Gospel had only been circulating in an oral manner throughout the Christian community. They would shortly become more formal Trinitarian and Christological heresies such as Arianism, Adoptionism, Docetism, Nestorianism, Pelagianism, Gnosticism, as well as several others which would later be more formally and specifically addressed by the early Church apologists and the ecumenical councils of Ephesus (431 AD), Chalcedon (451 AD), and Constantinople (680 AD).[4] The fact that John the Evangelist wrote his Gospel to defend belief in the divinity of Jesus as well as to endorse faith in his humanity by addressing the many heresies that arose was confirmed by many of the Church Fathers shortly after John wrote. We find evidence of this beginning with the church Father Ignatius of Antioch soon after John wrote his Gospel, in Ignatius' letters to the Ephesians and the Romans (110 AD). It is also found more definitively in the writings of the Church Father Irenaeus who was a disciple of John. Considerable evidence stating the intent of John's writing of his Gospel can be found throughout Irenaeus' five books addressed to the early Christian community which were called "Against Heresies" and written in about the year 174 AD.[5]

JOHN'S THEMATIC APPROACH-MAJOR AND SUB-THEMES

As far as taking the Gospel of John as a whole: The Gospel of John has traditionally been divided into four major themes, as well as several sub-themes which we will discuss in this book. The four major themes we will discuss first are continuous. They are found primarily in specific chapters of John's Gospel which is divided into four sections of concurrent chapters and they are:

1. The Prologue on the *Logos* (Chapter 1)
2. The Book of Signs (Chapters 2–12)
3. The Book of Glory (Chapters 13–20)
4. The Epilogue (Chapter 21)

Some of the sub-themes interspersed and threaded throughout the major themes we will discuss, and their locations scattered throughout this Gospel are:

a. The "I AM" Sayings (Jn 4:25–26; 6: 35, 41, 48, 51; 8: 12, 23–24, 28, 58; 10: 7, 9, 11, 14; 11: 25; 13: 19; 14: 6; 15: 1, 5).
b. Faith and Believing (Jn 1:7, 12, 50; 2:11, 22f; 3:12, 15f, 18, 36; 4:21, 39, 41f, 48, 50, 53; 5:24, 38, 44, 46f; 6:29f, 35f, 40, 47, 64, 69; 7:5, 31, 38f, 48; 8:24, 30f, 45f; 9:18, 35f, 38; 10:25f, 37f, 42; 11:15, 25ff, 40, 42, 45, 48; 12:11, 36ff, 42, 44, 46; 13:19; 14:1, 10ff, 29; 16:9, 27, 30f; 17:8, 20f; 19:35; 20:8, 25, 27, 29, 31).
c. Knowing and Unknowing (Jn 8:19; 13:1–11; 14:12–24; 15:17; 17:25–26).
d. Light and Darkness (Jn 1:4f, 7ff; 3:19ff; 5:35; 8:12; 9:5; 11:9f; 12:35f, 46).
e. Seeing and Blindness (Jn 1:49; 2:29; 3:1–12; 4: 15, 19, 25, 29, 42; 5:18; 7:1; 8:19, 31; 11:27; 19:38–39).
f. Ascent and Descent (Jn 1:32–33, 51; 3:13–18; 6:38, 53, 62; 8:23; 11:9; 13:1; 18:36; 20:17).
g. Life and Death (Jn 1:4; 3:14, 16, 36; 4:14; 5:24–26, 39; 6:27, 35, 40, 47–53, 63, 68; 8:12; 11:25; 14:6; 17:3; 20:31).
h. Love (Jn 3:16, 35; 8:42; 10:17; 11:3–5, 35–36; 12:25, 43; 13:1–35; 14:15–31; 15:9–19; 16:27; 17:23–26; Ch. 18–20; 19:26; 21:15–17).
i. Two Extended Allegories (Jn 10: 1–42; 15: 1–27).
j. Abiding and Discipleship (Jn 1:35–51; 3:30; 5:38; 6:56; 8:31–32; 12:34, 46; 13:34–35; 14:10,17; 15:1-8).
k. Spirit, Paraclete and Truth (Jn 1:9; 6:32; 7:38–39; Ch. 14:1–31; Ch.15:1–27; and Ch.16:1–33;18:36).

l. Bread and Water (Jn 3:5; 4:7–15; 5:1–18; 6:1–71; 7:37–39; 9:5–7; 13:1–17; 19:28, 34).
m. Son of Man-Son of God (Jn. 1:33–34, 49; 3:13–18; 8:28; 9:35; 10:30–36; 11:4, 25–27; 12:23, 34; 13:31–32; 14:13–14; 19: 7, 12; 20:30–31).
n. Judgment and the World (Jn. 3:16–19; 4:42; 5:22–24; 6:14, 33, 51; 7:4, 7; 8:12, 23, 26, 50; 9:5, 39; 11:9, 27; 12:31, 47–48; 14:17–19; 15:18; 16:7–11, 20, 28, 33; 17:4, 11–12; 18:20, 31, 36–37; 21:35).

By emphasizing a thematic approach and focusing on the divinity of Jesus as his launching point, John ended up composing a very different Gospel story. He employed simple, but highly symbolic language which made the finished work to be ultimately in stark contrast to the synoptic Gospels of Matthew, Mark, and Luke. Some examples are:

1. The symbolic words and language used in John are from common every-day experiences and the way John uses these words such as: word, light, life, bread, water, wind, world, lamb, fish, shepherd, hour, bread, vine, etc., enables them to embody a fuller, more pregnant meaning.
2. Much of the symbolism used by John will be used to show that in his front row seat to observing Him, nothing is considered unimportant in the life of Jesus Christ and what you sometime overlook is worth looking at more deeply.
3. In this Gospel there are also many dualistic images and contrasting opposites. For example, John's use of nouns and adverbs such as: light/darkness, life/death, above/below, spirit/flesh, truth/lies, etc.
4. In John, his themes draw out several "multiple meanings, considerable irony, and deeper truths." These themes seem to magnify all of these and render them incredibly filled with meaning.
5. The dialogues between Jesus and others often revolve around words and phrases that have not only multiple meanings but spiritual implications as well. The pattern is often the same: Jesus says something, one or more persons misunderstand him, and Jesus then brings the dialogue with the other person(s) to a deeper understanding. The misunderstanding often occurs because the other person(s) interprets Jesus' words on a literal, concrete, or physical level, whereas Jesus is really speaking on a more symbolic, abstract, or spiritual level. References to some of this dialogue is as follows:

"Destroy this temple, and in three days I will raise it up (Jn. 2:19-22)."

"I have food to eat which you do not know (Jn. 4:32-34)."

"I Am the bread which came down from heaven (Jn. 6: 41-51)."

"I Am the light of the world, whoever follows me will not walk in darkness (Jn. 8: 12)."

"Jesus said: 'I came into this world for judgment so that those who do not see may see, and those who do see may become blind' (Jn. 9:39-41)."

There are so many more that another entire book could be written just to discuss all of the many misunderstandings specifically. These word differences and the fuller understanding of their metaphorical meanings expressed through John's thematic approach end up making his Gospel far more abstract and somewhat obscure as opposed to the concreteness found in reading and understanding most of the words of the synoptic Gospels.

HISTORICAL-CRITICAL BIBLE STUDY METHOD

Before we get into discussing the many themes in John's Gospel, I'd like to talk briefly about the Bible study method that the Catholic church as well as several major Christian churches typically use today because it is very different than the Fundamentalist method used by some of the Evangelical Protestant churches. The Catholic church uses what is called the Historical-Critical method of studying the books of the Bible including, of course, The Gospel of John. Back in the late 1800's the Historical-Critical approach to Bible study was banned by the Holy See of the Catholic church who saw this approach as quite possibly a tool of Liberal Protestantism. That all changed in the year 1943 when the papal encyclical *Divino Afflante Spirito* was issued by Pope Pius XII. This encyclical encouraged the widespread study of the Bible by the faithful and found considerable merit in the utilization of the Historical-Critical method.[6]

Catholic scholar and theologian, Fr. Raymond Brown, was one of the forerunners of this approach and one of the first to apply this method to the entire Bible. He had been an editor of the Jerome Biblical Commentary, perhaps the most widely used and respected Catholic commentary on the entire Bible. Fr. Brown was also subsequently appointed as President of the Catholic Biblical Association and the Society of New Testament Studies. This method found universal acceptance as the approach the Catholic church would approve and adopt for use by Biblical scholars and Catholic theologians when Pope John XXIII convened Vatican Council II in 1962. Here in the council's "Dogmatic Constitution on Divine Revelation," *Dei Verbum,* this method found its universal acceptance for subsequent use throughout the church.[7]

WHAT IS THE HISTORICAL-CRITICAL METHOD?

This method looks at the language, style, time, location, culture and setting of when the words were supposedly written. It compares texts to other texts written around the same time. The truth lies in the historical context. It helps us to look beyond the texts and see the world in which a particular verse or some particular verses were actually written. Does that mean that it is still the Word of God? Of Course! But it looks at the Word of God as it was spoken through human persons who lived historically at a certain time and in a certain place within a certain culture. Doing this allows us to see for example, that Paul probably didn't write the Letter to the Hebrews and that it probably was a disciple of Paul who did. This method also allows us to look at the texts written in any book of the Bible according to what the words might mean instead of saying simply, "God said it, I believe it." As an example: if we were to read in any book written today that "It was raining cats and dogs," we would automatically understand that it was raining heavily and not that cats and dogs were literally falling from the sky, although we do believe that the Good Lord could miraculously do that if He wanted to.

On the other hand, some things in the Bible might have been meant to be taken literally and not figuratively or allegorically. The Historical-Critical Method enables us to sort out which is which. It seems that there is general agreement among most Catholic Biblical scholars that it was, in fact, John the apostle, the beloved disciple, who wrote most all of this Gospel in some form or fashion. The last chapter, Chapter 21, called the Epilogue most probably was an exception and a later addition to the rest of John's Gospel. The last chapter appears to have been added at a later date, either by John himself, his disciple, or someone who was a member of the early Christian church who was familiar with this Gospel. There is considerable evidence of redaction. We will talk about why this is probably the case when we employ the Historical-Critical approach to the texts and discuss the last chapter (Ch. 21) called "the Epilogue." The Historical-Critical method that the church currently uses allows us to determine that the bottom line here is that the last chapter probably was written at a later date than the first twenty chapters. The only outstanding question that will remain is by whom?

In studying the themes and sub-themes of John's Gospel, listen and look for words and word-pictures that John will use when we discuss words such as "light, life, true, see, believe, abide, and know." John will use them in a much fuller, dynamic, and vibrant sense than they are used in the synoptic tradition. Many of the words John uses in his Gospel and the manner in which he uses them don't really have any echo in the synoptic Gospels of Matthew, Mark, and Luke. The words "Logos" and "Paraclete" are prime examples. In fact, we don't find those words used anywhere else in the Bible. Ultimately, we will find that much of John's style of writing is far more comparable to the Wisdom tradition of Judaism as it was seen through the filter of Greek Hellenism than anything else. This style of writing combined the Jewish tradition with Greek culture, philosophy and thought. An example of where this can be seen vividly is in the *Logos* prologue of chapter one of John's Gospel. It appears to have many parallels found in the Old Testament Wisdom Books of Proverbs, Sirach, and the Book of Wisdom.

Finally, as was mentioned previously, a theme can be defined as a main idea, central thought, or an underlying message in any literary work. These themes may be stated directly or indirectly in any story; in John we will find both. The purpose of writing this book is to hopefully give the reader an understanding of the deeper meaning of John's Gospel, which in this author's opinion, might be grasped by gaining an understanding of his intended major themes and sub-themes. I hope that you have at least as much enjoyment interacting with John's underlying themes of his Gospel as I did in researching, discovering, and uncovering them, as well as subsequently preparing, compiling, and bringing the thematic material together cohesively to write this book.

NOTES

1. https://bible.usccb.org/bible/john/20:31

2. The Bible version which will be utilized as a reference throughout all the Chapters of this book will be The New American Bible as approved by the United States Council of Catholic Bishops. https://bible.usccb.org/bible/john/1. Catholic Church. (2001) United States Conference of Catholic Bishops USCCB. United States. Retrieved from the Library of Congress, https://www.loc.gov/item/lcwaN0008160/.

3. Healey, Mary, White, Sebastian ed., (Yonkers, NY, Magnificat Pub., 7/26/20) Magnificat Daily Meditation, p. 360.

4. "Church Councils," Knight Kevin, New Advent Catholic Encyclopedia online, (Ny, Ny, Robert Appleton Co., 1907), 28 Nov 2020 https://www.newadvent.org/library/almanac_14388a.htm

5. Peterson, John Bertram. "The Apostolic Fathers." The Catholic Encyclopedia. Vol. 1. (NY, New York: Robert Appleton Company, 1907). 28 Nov. 2020 http://www.newadvent.org/cathen/01637a.htm

6. Brown, Raymond, ed. Jerome Biblical Commentary, (Englewood Cliffs, NJ, Prentice Hall Publishing, 1969) Vatican Archives Online, http://www.vatican.va/archive/hist_councils/ii_vatican_council/index.htm

7. Ibid.

PART I

The Four Major Themes

Chapter 3

The Logos

The *Logos* is considered as the first of the four major themes in the Gospel of John. The description of who is the *Logos* occurs right at the opening of John in Chapter 1 vs. 1 to 18 which is called the Prologue. It sets the stage for everything else that is discussed in the Gospel.

THE *LOGOS* PROLOGUE

"In the beginning was the Word, and the Word was with God, and the Word was God. He was in the beginning with God. All things came to be through him, and without him nothing came to be. What came to be through him was life, and this life was the light of the human race; the light shines in the darkness, and the darkness has not overcome it. A man named John was sent from God. He came for testimony, to testify to the light, so that all might believe through him. He was not the light but came to testify to the light. The true light, which enlightens everyone, was coming into the world. He was in the world, and the world came to be through him, but the world did not know him. He came to what was his own, but his own people did not accept him. But to those who did accept him he gave power to become children of God, to those who believe in his name, who were born not by natural generation nor by human choice nor by a man's decision but of God. And the Word became flesh and made his dwelling among us, and we saw his glory, the glory as of the Father's only Son, full of grace and truth. John testified to him and cried out, saying, 'This was he of whom I said, "The one who is coming after me ranks ahead of me because he existed before me."' From his fullness we have all received, grace in place of grace, because while the law was given through Moses, grace and truth came through Jesus Christ. No one has ever seen God. The only Son, God, who is at the Father's side, has revealed him (Jn. 1:1–18)."[1]

Chapter 3

EVOLUTION OF THE TERM

The term, "*Logos*" was NOT first used by John, the Evangelist. It was a philosophic term used by philosophers and theologians and was percolating in the ancient world long before John wrote his Gospel. In addition to the Greeks, the term can also be found threaded throughout several centuries of Persian, Indian, and Egyptian culture and thought. The idea of the *logos* in Greek thought predates John's use of the term by about six centuries. It can be traced as far back as the philosopher Heraclitus who was seen to be the first of the Greek philosophers to have written about it. He equated the *logos* with fire and saw it as a universal principle controlling the cosmos and ruling the world. Coincidently, he wrote from Ephesus where John, the Evangelist resided. He is said to have written a single book (papyrus roll) which he deposited in the Temple of Artemis at Ephesus as there were no known libraries which existed at that time. One of Heraclitus' first recorded statements about the *logos* found in this book was as follows: "Having harkened not to me but to the Word (*Logos*) it is wise to agree that all things are one."[2]

The term then saw many evolutions of Greek thought following this and although John's use of the term will be different in its application, he will need to address what the term "*logos*" meant to the Hellenistic world before and at the time of his writing of the Gospel. In philosophy, the term's use in classical Greek thought referred to a universal divine reason which was immanent in nature yet transcended all opposing forces and imperfections in the entire cosmos and humanity. It was also described as an eternal and unchanging truth present in the universe from the time of creation and was available to every individual who sought it, though few if any attained it. As the term "*logos*" evolved in Greek philosophy, it was used by the Stoics about four centuries before John's Gospel and then is found in the writings of Plato and Aristotle as well as several other philosophers leading up to the Jewish philosopher Philo. He used the term and wrote just a few decades before John the Evangelist. In early Hebrew thought the *logos* had been equated with the God of creation who made all things by His Word (Gn. 1:3), and later found a parallel with the personification of Wisdom (Wi. 9:1–2).[3]

Philo lived in Alexandria which at that time was an Egyptian province of Rome. Philo was thoroughly educated in Greek philosophy and culture as can be seen from his superb knowledge of classical Greek literature. He is seen by many to be the forerunner of Christian theology in his attempt to synthesize and reconcile the Jewish faith with Hellenistic philosophy. His works combined the writings of Plato and Moses into one philosophical system. Philo regarded the Hebrew Bible as the source not only of religious revelation, but also of all philosophic truth. To Philo, the *logos* was God's creative principle and the mediating idea between God and the world. *Logos* is neither uncreated as God is, nor created as men are but occupied a middle position. Philo pictured the *logos* as having the function of an advocate on behalf of humanity and as God's envoy to the world. We should state here emphatically again that the way the term *logos* was used up to the time of John the Evangelist was strictly as a philosophical idea to describe in general terms something on the order of the soul of the universe or to describe divine reason or understanding or divine intelligence or principle. The *logos* to Philo and other Jewish and Greek philosophers and theologians of the time was understood as the plan in the mind of God which was believed to have given the cosmos its form and its meaning. Following the Jewish mythical tradition, Philo represents the *logos* as the utterance of God found in the Jewish scripture of the Old Testament since God's word does not differ from his actions. The fundamental doctrine propounded by Philo is that of *logos* as an intermediary power, a messenger and mediator between God and the world. Ultimately, Philo will view the *logos* as the first-born Son of God stating that the *logos* has an origin but as God's thought it also has eternal generation. It exists as such before everything else all of which are secondary products of God's thought. Therefore, it is called the "first-born." The *logos* is thus more than a quality, power, or characteristic of God; it is an entity eternally generated as an extension to which Philo ascribes many names and functions, not the least of which being that: "The *Logos* is the first-begotten Son of the Uncreated Father."[4]

One point that needs to be made clear, however, is that Philo never imagined the *logos* to ever be an actual person. Philo's *logos* is impersonal, an idea, a power, and though occasionally identified with the angels of the Bible or the Son of the Father, this is by no more than symbolic personification. What will be dramatically different here is how the Gospel writer John will use "Logos," as much more than just a philosophical term, but none the less, John was colored certainly by Philo as well as several preceding influences in Hellenistic philosophy and in other surrounding cultures. Granted that John is using a term that was familiar to the readers of his day, but when John asserts as he does in his Gospel that: "The Word/*Logos* became flesh and dwelt among us (Jn.1:14)." He is indeed saying something that was radically different and never dreamt of by any of the line of Greek, Jewish, or other philosophers who lived and wrote before John wrote his Gospel.

THE *LOGOS* IN JOHN

John's *Logos* Prologue is at once mystical, profound, poetic, and prophetic. The *Logos* term to describe Jesus will appear only in John's Gospel and nowhere is it used in any of the other three Gospels. In fact, nowhere is it ever used anywhere else in the entire Bible; it may be implied, but never used. Although the term "Logos" or Word is not repeated as a title in John's Gospel beyond the prologue, the entire Gospel of John is written to lay out some basic claims concerning the *Logos*. Here are some of those claims in John:

1. As the *Logos*, Jesus Christ is pre-existent and God in self-revelation and redemption.
2. As the *Logos*, He became flesh and dwelt among men in the person of Jesus of Nazareth.
3. As the *Logos*, Jesus Christ not only gives God's Word to us as humans; He is the Word.
4. As the *Logos*, Jesus is not only God revealing; He is God revealed.
5. As the *Logos*, He is God to the extent that he can be present to man and knowable to man.
6. As the *Logos*, this term will be of utmost importance in our coming to believe in the divinity of Jesus as God-Man.
7. As the *Logos*, Jesus is God in person and that the Father, the Son, and the Holy Spirit together are three persons but one God.

But who and what is the *Logos* and what did the term mean both to John, as well as to the early Christian community? First, "Word" is the best English translation we can render for the Greek term *Logos* as used by John, but the intention certainly is to convey more than word as what we understand as an item used in speech or part of language. For anyone reading or hearing his Gospel, John wanted us to believe that Jesus was the very incarnation and manifestation of God-divine reason, divine wisdom and intelligence, divine action, divine persona and substance, the divinity of God in human form. To John, Jesus is the divine being in Himself, the very Son of God and the author of creation. The *Logos* is God in action, creating, revealing, saving, and redeeming. But the *Logos*, is not only God revealing; the *Logos* is also God revealed in Jesus. The Christ event is of great significance because through it, the Word became flesh, a human being.

In the *Logos* prologue, John will introduce Jesus as God's being and persona. In doing this John will be merging and incorporating all previous Hebrew biblical faith throughout Israel's history and synthesizing it with Greek philosophical thought of the time and the milieu he lived in. Many

Biblical scholars have called the *Logos* the KEY theme of John's Gospel. As the Gospel opens, here is what John says in the first few verses:

> In the beginning was the Word, and the Word was with God, and the Word was God. He was with God in the beginning. Through him all things were made; without him nothing was made that has been made... (and down to verse 14) "The Word became flesh and made his dwelling among us (Jn. 1:1, 14)."

John the Evangelist interprets the *Logos* as inseparable from the person of the pre-existent, eternal Jesus, the Son of God. In effect, that Jesus does not simply proclaim the Gospel of God, but that Jesus IS the Gospel of God. It is not unintentional on John's part that his Prologue on the *Logos* begins by paralleling the opening of the book of Genesis: "In the beginning God created the heavens and the earth (Gn. 1:1)."

It is believed that this was certainly intentional on John's part. The Word here points directly to Genesis 1, where the act of creation is the effect of God speaking. God, who is in His own nature hidden, revealing himself in creation, is the root of the Logos-idea, in contrast with all materialistic or pantheistic conceptions of creation. This idea develops itself in The Word becoming a human being, embodying the divine will and the divine person as it was previously used in Hebrew poetry. Consequently, divine attributes are predicated of it as being the continuous revelation and self-communication of God.

The previous Old Testament idea of wisdom being hidden and then revealed as being a divine person is also carried forth here in the term *Logos*. Throughout the history of Hebrew thought, wisdom would be the pre-existent divine agent who draws man to God and is identified with the word of God. The associating of God with Divine Wisdom is seen as one of the characteristics inherent in God's creative activity. It was during the time of the writing of the Wisdom Literature (c. 500 BC) that the personification of wisdom had begun. It was then that wisdom would be portrayed as a pre-existent person, God's first person, with prophetic, divine, and messianic traits, who would stand apart from God Himself. She would be seen to have an intermediate role in creation and in the government and ordering of the universe. References to the personification of Divine Wisdom are found first in the Book of Job chapter 28:12–18, then more particularly in the Book of Proverbs, chapters 1–9, the Book of Sirach chapter 24, and the Book of Wisdom chapters 7–9.

What had been said in the Wisdom literature of the Old Testament concerning the personification of Divine Wisdom is also then being incorporated by John to describe the person of Jesus as the *Logos*. Here are some examples:

1. Wisdom's origins are divine (Pr. 8:22; Si 24:3,9; Wi 7:25–26).

2. Wisdom is pre-existent and had a role in creation (Pr. 8:22–29; Si. 1:4, 9, 10; Wi. 7:22; 8:4–6, 9:9).
3. Wisdom is identified with the Spirit of God and immanent in the world (Wi. 1:7, 7:24, 8:1, 9:17, 12:1).
4. Wisdom has a particular mission to human beings (Pr. 8:4, 31–36; Si. 24:7, 12, 19–22; Wi. 7:27–28; 8:2–3).
5. Wisdom speaks to human beings in the world (Pr. 1, 8, 9; Si. 24:19–22; Wi. 6:12–16, 7:22, 8:7–9, 9:10–16).
6. Wisdom promises life and blessings (Pr. 1:32, 3:13–18, 8:1–5, 9:1–6; Si. 1:14–20, 6:18–31; Wi. 7:7–14).
7. Wisdom is a gift from God to humanity and the world (Pr. 2:6; Si. 1:9–10; Wi. 7:7, 9:4).
8. Wisdom is associated particularly with Israel (Si. 24:8–23; Ba. 4:1; Wi. 10:1–21).
9. Wisdom is a person and is personified (Jb. 28; Pr. 1–9–10, 4:11–19, 6:18–31, 14:20-15:8; Ba. 3:9-4:4; Wi. 6:12-11:1).
10. Wisdom is seen as the breath of God who reflects eternal light shining in the present while reflecting both the past and the future; she is pure, sinless, undefiled, and is the very image of God (Wi. 7:24–26).

In the earlier Old Testament writings, wisdom, (*hokmah,* Hb.) had become mostly identified with the law. But, at the time that John the Evangelist is writing his Gospel, the Jewish faith was being influenced considerably by Hellenistic thought. Wisdom, (*hokmah,* Hb.) becomes more influenced, familiarized, and synthesized with the wisdom of Hellenism (*sophia,* Gk.). Therefore, in some regard, the Word, (*Logos,* Gk.) will also imply that Jesus is not only the fullness of all intelligible reality and Son of God, but also the personification of wisdom as well. Therefore, *Logos,* the Word, would ultimately have a more "pregnant" meaning. I'm sure you realize that Judaism was a very Patriarchal culture, so it may interest you to know that in the Old Testament of the Bible, the persona of Wisdom was always described as a "SHE." Don't let that mislead you. Remember that the Bible opens by saying: "God made them in his own image, male and female he created them (Gn. 1:27)." God's image is the complete fullness of all that we understand to be male and female and as the *Logos,* Jesus is not only fully human and fully divine but the fullness of God's image as well.

The Prologue has been seen by some as a "Great Hymn" or a "Great Poem," but it also is certainly much more than this. On the other hand, some scholars believe that the Prologue was an already existing liturgical hymn to wisdom which John adopted for his purposes. There will be many other themes expressed later in John's Gospel which are first introduced in this Prologue such as light, darkness, life, faith, belief, love, and truth. These several sub-themes will be more fully developed throughout the Gospel of John. Therefore, this Prologue is key and can be considered as the springboard into John's more complete description of Jesus as the *Logos* by later expanding on many of these sub-themes he first mentions in the Prologue. Here, John will introduce Jesus as the Son of God to the ancient Hebrew/Greek community. As was stated earlier, Greek philosophy as well as the early Hebrew theologian and philosopher, Philo and others may have used the term *logos*, as a reference to divine reason or divine mind, but John will use it very differently to note many of the attributes of Jesus who IS God. In John's use of the term, we find in the Prologue that:

- Jesus is eternal ("In the beginning was the Word Jn. 1:1")
- Jesus was pre-existent and with God prior to coming to earth ("the Word was with God Jn. 1:1")
- Jesus is God ("the Word was God Jn. 1:1")
- Jesus is Creator and was there at creation ("All things were made through him Jn. 1:2")
- Jesus is the Giver of Life ("In him was life Jn. 1:3")
- Jesus is the Light ("His life was the light of men and the light shines in the darkness Jn. 1:6–9")
- Jesus is the Glory of God ("glory as of the only Son from the Father Jn. 1:14–15")
- Jesus became human to live among us ("the Word became flesh and dwelt among us Jn. 1:14"), and finally
- Jesus is seeable and knowable. ("No one has ever seen God; the only God, who is at the Father's side, he has made him known Jn. 1:18") The Word, John says, was both "with God" (distinct from God the Father) and "was God" (fully God) (Jn. 1:1).

If the Jehovah Witnesses have ever come to your door, you have found that this verse the way it should be translated, gives a very different understanding than the way they translate it. The Jehovah Witnesses believe that it should be translated as: "The Word was a god."[5]
They add the "a" giving the mistaken understanding that Jesus was one of many gods. It should be accurately translated from the Greek or Aramaic ancient languages as: "The Word was God (Jn. 1:1)."

The Word's true deity is confirmed through his identification as the Creator of all things (Jn.1:3).

Though fully divine, Jesus enters human existence when: "the Word became flesh and made his dwelling among us (Jn. 1:14)."

The reason for this incarnation was to bring people back into right relationship with God and to make them "children of God" by faith (JN. 1:12). How does this happen? A few verses later we find out. The middle portion of the Prologue introduces John the Baptist, a man who is sent from God, who came as a witness to the true Light (Jn. 1:6–8), which enlightens every man, coming into the world (Jn. 1:9–13). Jesus will identify himself later in John's Gospel as the "Light of the world" in John 9:5. John 1:12 conveys that we, through believing in Jesus as the true Light which has come into the world, have the power to become children of God by faith in His name, being born not by blood, flesh or will. The capstone to the Prologue is as follows:

> No one has ever seen God, but the one and only Son, who is himself God and is in closest relationship with the Father, has made him known (Jn. 1:18).

Jesus who is God-Man, makes known the hidden and invisible God. Here, the Prologue returns to eternity in the final verse as the Son reveals the Father. There is a continuous action expressed indicating the eternal presence of the Son which began in the bosom of the Father. Following the Prologue, the scene returns to earth again beginning in verse 19 with John the Baptist baptizing, giving testimony, making straight the way of the Lord, and then pointing to the "Lamb of God," The *Agnus Dei*, a description of Jesus, which, like the *Logos,* appears only in John's writings (Jn.1:29). We will find later in this Gospel that The Lamb of God title bestowed on Jesus by John the Baptist at the beginning of his earthly ministry would indicate that the divine Jesus, the *Logos*, would choose to suffer crucifixion as a sign of his full obedience to the will of his divine Father. He would be the Lamb of God and servant of God who would pick up his cross and carry away our sins and the sin of the world. In the words of French spiritual author, Fr. Jean Du Coeur De Jesus D' Elbee, this is referred to as the "Sublime Exchange," which he describes as: "My sins on Him, His blood on me."[6]

The sacrifice of the lamb would lead to eventual victory in the resurrection. Later, in the Book of Revelation/The Apocalypse, John would include no less than twenty-nine references to a "lion-like lamb" who would be slain but standing and who would deliver victory in a manner reminiscent of the resurrected Christ. What follows is just one of those many references to the "lion-like lamb" from John's Book of Revelation; Ch. 5:1–13:

> I saw a scroll in the right hand of the one who sat on the throne. It had writing on both sides and was sealed with seven seals. Then I saw a mighty angel who proclaimed in a loud voice, "Who is worthy to open the scroll and break its seals?" But no one in heaven or on earth or under the earth was able to open the scroll or to examine it. I shed many tears because no one was found worthy to open the scroll or to examine it. One of the elders said to me, "Do not weep. The lion of the tribe of Judah, the root of David, has triumphed, enabling him to open the scroll with its seven seals." Then I saw standing, in the midst of the throne

and the four living creatures and the elders, a Lamb that seemed to have been slain. He had seven horns and seven eyes; these are the [seven] spirits of God sent out into the whole world. He came and received the scroll from the right hand of the one who sat on the throne. When he took it, the four living creatures and the twenty-four elders fell down before the Lamb. Each of the elders held a harp and gold bowls filled with incense, which are the prayers of the holy ones. They sang a new hymn: "Worthy are you to receive the scroll and to break open its seals, for you were slain and with your blood you purchased for God those from every tribe and tongue, people and nation. You made them a kingdom and priests for our God, and they will reign on earth." I looked again and heard the voices of many angels who surrounded the throne and the living creatures and the elders. They were countless in number, and they cried out in a loud voice: "Worthy is the Lamb that was slain to receive power and riches, wisdom and strength, honor and glory and blessing." Then I heard every creature in heaven and on earth and under the earth and in the sea, everything in the universe, cry out: "To the one who sits on the throne and to the Lamb be blessing and honor, glory and might, forever and ever" (Rv. 5: 1-13).

Again, in Christian theology both the Word, *Logos* and the Lamb of God, *Agnus Dei* are distinct titles for Jesus found only in John and they are viewed as foundational and integral to the message of Christianity.

CHRISTOLOGY

Before we conclude our discussion on the theme of the *Logos*, the first of the four major themes, let me say something briefly about what is called "Christology" because an understanding of Christology might help us to see and understand more clearly why John's Gospel is so different from the synoptic Gospels of Matthew, Mark, and Luke. What is Christology? It is the study of Jesus Christ: The study of Jesus' natures, person, ministry, and consciousness. There is frequently understood to be two ways for anyone to study Christology. The first way is called "Christology from below" (low Christology). Here, one starts with the Jesus of history and shows how Jesus' earthly birth and life is significant for our salvation. The synoptic Gospels of Matthew, Mark, and Luke are examples of what is called, "Christology from below."

The other way for anyone to study Christology is called "Christology from above" (high Christology). Here, one starts with the *Logos*, the very Word of God in heaven, the divine Jesus, and then views Jesus as "The Word" who came down to earth from on high for our salvation. The starting point for studying Christology is different with each one. The Gospel of John and many of Paul's letters are examples of "Christology from above" or high

Christology. We will talk more about the subject of Christology when we get to the Sub-theme Ascent and Descent in John's Gospel later in the book.[7]

THE TRINITY

I would also like to say a few words about the Trinity which hopefully will help our understanding of the *Logos*. It would be about another 150 years after John wrote his Gospel that the *Logos*, the Word, would then be widely seen as part of what would become a developing Trinitarian Theology. It began with the writings of the early Christian theologians, namely Justin Martyr, Irenaeus, Clement of Alexandria, Polycarp, Basil, and Tertullian giving testimony to the truths of the Christian faith. Then the Christian theology of the *Logos* as being the person of Jesus, the Son of God, and part of the Trinity worked itself through the early church councils of the fourth century, particularly the Nicean Council of 325 AD, under the Christian emperor Constantine. From this council originated the beginnings of what we know now as the Nicean Creed, i.e., that:

> We believe in one God, the Father, almighty, maker of heaven and earth, that we believe in one Lord Jesus Christ, the only begotten Son of God, and that we believe in the Holy Spirit, the Lord, the giver of life.[8]

Later, the Council of Chalcedon in 451 declared that Jesus possessed full divinity along with full humanity. Following the writings of Eusebius and Athanasius who defended the divinity of Jesus against the Arian and Nestorian heresies as well as others, the Doctrine of the Trinity wound its way through the many subsequent church councils and into what was called the Athanasian Creed of the sixth century which defended the Doctrine of the Trinity and particularly the divinity of Jesus Christ, The *Logos*. Then followed the words of the Athanasian Creed which declared: "the Father is God, the Son is God, and the Holy Spirit is God, and yet there are not three Gods but one God."[9]

In this Trinity of Persons, the Son is begotten of the Father by an eternal generation, and the Holy Spirit proceeds by an eternal procession from the Father and the Son. The Persons of the Trinity are co-eternal and co-equal. All three Persons are uncreated and omnipotent. Father, Son and Holy Spirit are in complete harmony of Being as well as in harmony of Divine Mind and Divine Will. This is essentially the revelation of God which we call the Trinity. The revelation regards God's nature which Jesus Christ, the Son of God, came upon the earth as the Word, the *Logos,* to deliver to the world. The *Logos* came to earth both as the revealer and as God revealed. The bottom line is, after John wrote his Gospel, the early church and growing Christian community took some time in considering the *Logos* to be a person, as well as THE person of Jesus and Jesus to be God in person. John's intention for the *Logos* to be seen in the person of Jesus would later evolve and eventually become Trinitarian Theology – The *Logos* would be a divine person who was part of an eternal Godhead consisting of three persons in one God, Father, Son, and Holy Spirit.

At this point, we hopefully have some idea of what John meant by using the term *Logos* to describe Jesus, who is the God-Man, but as far as having an in-depth understanding of the Trinity, most theologians would agree that even when you think you understand the Trinity, you don't. That says I don't and you don't even if we think we do. We can talk about the Trinity and discuss it in language. For example, we can describe the Trinity as being like a shamrock with three corners on the one leaf or of water taking the three forms of liquid, ice, and steam, but even when we can talk about the Trinity and discuss it in the most profound theological language, it will all end up being merely the language of metaphor. The Trinity will end up being "like" something. This is because the Trinity is revealed to us as a "mystery." The Vatican Council has explained the meaning to be attributed to the term "mystery" in theology. It defines the word, "mystery" in this way: "A mystery is a truth which we are not merely incapable of discovering apart from Divine Revelation, but which, even when revealed, remains 'hidden by the veil of faith and enveloped, so to speak, by a kind of darkness.'"[10]

Finally, it is Jesus, the *Logos* (Word) through the illuminating action of the Holy Spirit, present in us and in the church, who witnesses to and instructs us in all Divine Mystery including the mystery of the Holy Trinity. Let's just leave this one and say that its difficult enough to try to understand how Jesus is the *Logos*, let alone to try to understand the Trinity. Part of our Christian Faith, however, means believing even though we might not fully understand. So, as Catholics and as Christians, we can have a developing understanding of the *Logos* as the Gospel writer John had described Jesus. As a result of that understanding of the *Logos,* it can then lead to our having a firmer foundation for belief in Divine Mystery including the Holy Trinity. But after that, it is best to just leave the reality of the Trinity at its home which is located somewhere in mystery.

In conclusion, one wonders if we would have ever even had a developed doctrine of the Trinity as a foundation for our Christian belief were it not for the writing of John's Gospel and his *Logos* Prologue. Lastly, it should be of note that following the *Logos* Prologue in Chapter 1, John the Evangelist never uses the term again in the remainder of his Gospel nor in any of his three Epistles. He does, however, make one other lone reference to the *Logos* in the Book of Revelation he wrote from prison on the isle of Patmos:

His eyes were [like] a fiery flame, and on his head were many diadems. He had a name inscribed that no one knows except himself. He wore a cloak that had been dipped in blood, and his name was called the Word of God (Rv. 19:12-13).

NOTES

1. Ibid 2 Chapter Two.
2. B50, "Heraclitus," Zalta, Edward, (Stanford Enc. Of Phil., Scholarly Publishing and Resources Coalition, Online Version, 1999).
3. Ibid Ch. 3 no. 2, https://plato.stanford.edu/contents.html
4. Sacr. 8; Somn. 1.182; Op13, http://www.iep.utm.edu/philo/#H11).
5. https://www.jw.org/en/library/bible/
6. https://deaconconlin.com/2015/05/12/i-believe-in-love-a-personal-retreat-based-on-the-teaching-of-st-therese-of-lisieux-by-fr-jean-c-j-delbee/
7. "Jesus Christ," Karl Rahner, Encyclopedia of Theology, A Concise Sacramentum Mundi, (Ny, NY, Burns and Oates Pub, 2004).
8. https://www.catholic.org/prayers/prayer.php?p=495
9. https://www.ccel.org/creeds/athanasian.creed.html
10. Ibid 1 Chapter 2, Vatican II Constitution, *De Fide,* Cath IV.

Chapter 4

The Book of Signs

SIGN, SYMBOL, SACRAMENT

A sign points to, leads to, or indicates something or someone which is not immediately apparent. In effect, it stands for or signifies someone or something else and in doing so conveys meaning. Signs are constituted with meaning and can be natural or supernatural. The former is based on human reason and the latter transcends reason and is based on mystery and divine revelation. In the Gospel of John, the actual distinction between a natural and supernatural sign is tenuous at best. The signs in John occur at the intersection of reality and mystery, and Jesus will use the signs to reveal himself to his disciples, to the crowd, and to the world.

In the New Testament, the word "miracle" is not used at all. The Greek word used for "sign" is *"semeion,"* and if the sign is considered as miraculous, the word used in the Greek is *"teras"* which is translated as "wonder." In the Gospel of John, the meaning of the word "sign" is nuanced and is often used to indicate an unaccustomed, extraordinary, amazing, and unexpected event which serves as a motive for belief and credibility by manifesting the power of God. When it is Christ performing the sign, it creates belief in his person and conveys evidence of Jesus' divinity (ex. Jn. 2:11). Surely, each of the seven signs are a miracle. They cannot be seen within a closed system governed by rigid natural law when it is the interference with so-called "natural law" that actually makes the sign a miracle.

A "symbol" (*symbaleo,* Gk.) is a form of a visible sign that often may have a deeper invisible and hidden meaning. A symbol is something that represents something else. The visible reality represents an invisible reality while both the visible and invisible maintain their own separate realities. The cross of Christ, for example, is both a sign and a symbol. Also, in the Eucharist, the bread and wine continue to be bread and wine visibly though they transform and become an invisible reality, the body and blood of Christ. Beyond being a sign and a symbol, the Eucharist is also a Sacrament as it was instituted by Christ and entrusted to the church as a sign of grace. A Sacrament then, is considered as a sign of grace through which God conveys and we receive a sharing in the life of God through the action of the Holy Spirit. For the first eleven centuries of the Christian church the word "sacrament" (*mysterion*, Gk.; *sacramentum,* L.), did not designate a rite as we know it (Sacrament). The word "sacrament," had a much broader meaning as something sacred or hidden. All reality is imbued with the hidden presence of God. Therefore, in this world, many material things are signs of something spiritual and sacred. In this broader sense of the word then, all of Jesus' signs were not only symbols, but were sacramental in that they were visible grace-filled signs of a deeper, spiritual, mysterious, and invisible reality.

THE SEVEN SIGNS

In Hebrew thought, the number seven is considered a perfect number as it constitutes completion and perfection, physically and spiritually. The basis of this number representing perfection was originally derived from the Book of Genesis (Gn. 1:1, 27). Subsequently, we are told that on the seventh day, God blessed it, made it holy, and on this day, God rested from all the work of creation. So, to John it is no coincidence that in his Gospel, Jesus will perform seven signs. Additionally, when the Evangelist John will later write the Book of Revelation/The Apocalypse, he will write to seven churches (Rv. 1:4), there are seven seals (Rv. 6:1–7:8), seven angels (Rv. 8:2), seven trumpets of God (Rv. 8:1–11:19), seven thunders (Rv. 10: 3–4), seven last plagues (Rv. 15:1–18:20), and seven bowls (Rv. 16:1). It is the blowing of the seventh trumpet in the Book of Revelation that will initiate the first resurrection from the dead, hence bringing perfection and completion to salvation brought by Jesus Christ.

In the Book of Signs, it is interesting to note that Jesus never calls any of the seven His "signs" *(semeion, Gk.),* or even His "miracles" (*terga, dynamis*, Gk.). Jesus will call these seven, His "works" (*ergon,* Gk.). In the Book of Signs, the second of the major themes (John Chapters 2 to 12), we find seven notable and miraculous events which are recorded by the Gospel writer. All seven signs will be used to point to the ultimate sign, which is to follow—the resurrection of Jesus Christ from the dead. This ultimate sign will prove beyond any shadow of a doubt that Jesus is the Sacrament of God. The seven signs performed by Jesus will all be linked together continuously in Chapters 2–12 to both reveal Jesus' divinity as well as to manifest the imminent inbreaking of the Kingdom of God into history. There will be seen to be dominion over nature and natural law in the world and over human nature as well. Because the Kingdom of God is present within Jesus, He will be able to show how He is mysteriously in control of nature as nature will obey the commands of Jesus. The wonder of the signs as miracles is that a natural outcome or effect is expected other than what actually takes place. The ordinary course of the laws of nature (reality) are transformed by Jesus into the extraordinary (mystery). Jesus' signs or miracles will transcend nature and are outside of what we consider as reality. In that they are all shrouded in mystery, they are supernatural and the experience of the disciples and the spectators cannot even be called "surreal" as the signs are more "trans-real." On the other hand, none of the disciples and no one in the crowd who follows Jesus can label them as "unreal" or "unnatural." The signs are, in effect, Jesus' reality.

The seven signs and the resurrection which follows them will point to Jesus as the primordial Sacrament of God as Jesus will prove himself to be the ultimate sign. There will be no dichotomy between nature and grace, natural and supernatural, divinity and humanity, heaven and earth. The transcendent will be made visible in the imminent and the eternal made visible in that historical moment in time. The signs should all be considered as "sacramental" in that they are all visible signs of grace; namely the signs are imbued with the divine presence of God. The Kingdom of God which will be gradually seen by the disciples and later seen by many as present within Jesus will be the evidential reality as to how and why the Kingdom of God is truly in our midst. In the Book of Signs, seven signs are listed, but we will be told at the end of the Gospel that Jesus performed many more than seven, but seven signs are recorded. Jumping ahead to the end of John's Gospel, he is going to leave a key to the signs for us at the back door so to speak. John will tell us:

> There are many other signs Jesus did in the presence of His disciples—but these are written so that you may believe that Jesus is the Christ, the Son of God, and that believing you may have life through His Name (Jn. 20.30-31).[1]

So, at the end of his Gospel, John will tell us that even though there were many more signs the disciples witnessed, these seven signs (a perfect number of signs) were particularly recorded by him so that we might believe that Jesus is the Christ, the Son of God, and that if we believe, we might have life through His Name.

The way Matthew, Mark, and Luke saw the meaning and intention of Jesus' signs were somewhat different than the way John saw them. For example, in terms of the role that faith played the synoptic Gospel writers emphasized faith as a prerequisite for Jesus to perform the sign in the first place. In John, however, people often come to faith and belief as a result of seeing the sign. Furthermore, in the synoptics, the signs or miracles are performed to show Jesus' authority. In John, they are proofs of Jesus' origin, identity, and relationship to God as God's Son. Regardless of why they were performed by

Jesus, I think we would agree that the signs were important just the same as many signs we see all around us are important. For example, road signs such as "Turn Here," "55 MPH," "Detour"-these signs direct our way and try to keep us out of harm's way. Other signs such as "EXIT," "STOP," "One Way," "No Smoking," etc., may tell us what we should or should not do or point the way for us.

The original Greek word for "sign" (*semeion*) was eventually translated into the Latin word *signum* from which we ultimately get our English word "sign." In the Book of Signs, John will refer to these seven signs as coming from heaven. Through these seven signs, Jesus will begin to reveal Himself to the world and to his followers. Through these signs, Jesus will begin to show not only God revealing, but also God revealed in His person. Following the Book of Signs, the third major theme in John's Gospel which is called the Book of Glory, will begin and run from Chapter 13 through Chapter 20. We will discuss the Book of Glory after learning more about the individual seven events in this section of John's Gospel which are called seven signs. The seven signs recorded in John's Book of Signs are:

1. Changing water into wine at Cana, Jn. 2:1–11 - "the first of the signs"
2. Healing the royal official's son in Capernaum, Jn. 4:46–54
3. Healing the paralytic at Bethesda, Jn. 5:1–15
4. Feeding the 5000, Jn. 6:5–14
5. Jesus walking on water, Jn. 6:16–24
6. Healing the man blind from birth, Jn. 9:1–7
7. The raising of Lazarus, Jn. 11:1–45

Let's look at each of the seven signs in more detail.

First Sign-The Changing of the Water into Wine at the Wedding in Cana (Jn. 2:1–11)

> On the third day there was a wedding in Cana in Galilee, and the mother of Jesus was there. Jesus and his disciples were also invited to the wedding. When the wine ran short, the mother of Jesus said to him, "They have no wine." And Jesus said to her, "Woman, how does your concern affect me? My hour has not yet come." His mother said to the servers, "Do whatever he tells you." Now there were six stone water jars there for Jewish ceremonial washings, each holding twenty to thirty gallons. Jesus told them, "Fill the jars with water." So, they filled them to the brim. Then he told them, "Draw some out now and take it to the headwaiter." So, they took it. And when the headwaiter tasted the water that had become wine, without knowing where it came from (although the servers

who had drawn the water knew), the headwaiter called the bridegroom and said to him, "Everyone serves good wine first, and then when people have drunk freely, an inferior one; but you have kept the good wine until now." Jesus did this as the beginning of his signs in Cana in Galilee and so revealed his glory, and his disciples began to believe in him (Jn.2: 1-11).

Only the Gospel of John mentions the wedding at Cana with Jesus turning the water into wine. Because of the High Christology emphasized in the Gospel of John, the marriage celebrated at the wedding at Cana, in a mystical sense, may have been seen by John to signify Christ's divinity with Jesus being seen figuratively as the bridegroom and the early Christian church as the bride. It was the role of Mary, Mother of God, to ask for what would become this first sign or miracle. Jesus' role would be to perform His works and the role of the disciples would be twofold: to be the witnesses and then to believe that Jesus is not just Messiah, but the Son of God, The Word of God become flesh. In this first sign, Jesus will tell us as He tells Mother Mary that: "His hour had not yet come." We are first being reminded here that even though the hour for Jesus' mission was not upon Him, (i.e. to be crucified and glorified), it was not too far off. This sign will show that Jesus has power over nature which only God possesses.

What usually takes a vineyard and a vineyard grower months and months to produce after cultivation, Jesus will transform water into wine immediately at the wedding as a favor to His mother. To perform this sign Jesus will use a simple and common everyday thing, like water as a representation of that which cleanses, purifies, and quenches thirst to be transformed immediately into wine which is a sign of celebration. This is an important sign, not only because it is the first one shown, but also because Jesus' hour of crucifixion, like the water, will cleanse and purify us and show that those coming to Him will never thirst.

The wine being transformed from the water will be a sign of Jesus' resurrection, a sign of celebration and joy, with similarity to a wedding celebration. Occurring at a humble village wedding at the request of His mother, this the first sign, is a sign of Jesus' visible glory spoken of in the *Logos* Prologue of Chapter one where it was said: "We beheld His Glory, glory as of the only Son from the Father (Jn. 1:14)."

John is also having Jesus show us here that even though Jesus' hour had not yet come, he can perform some miracles at the request of those who love Him. I was not there but I can imagine Jesus maybe even rolling his eyes at His mother's request and possibly saying: "Oh, Mother, please; you want me to do this now?"

Second Sign-Healing of the Royal Official's Son (Jn. 4:46–54)

> Then he returned to Cana in Galilee, where he had made the water wine. Now there was a royal official whose son was ill in Capernaum. When he heard that Jesus had arrived in Galilee from Judea, he went to him and asked him to come down and heal his son, who was near death. Jesus said to him, "Unless you people see signs and wonders, you will not believe." The royal official said to him, "Sir, come down before my child dies." Jesus said to him, "You may go; your son will live." The man believed what Jesus said to him and left. While he was on his way back, his slaves met him and told him that his boy would live. He asked them when he began to recover. They told him, "The fever left him yesterday, about one in the afternoon." The father realized that just at that time Jesus had said to him, "Your son will live," and he and his whole household came to believe. Now this was the second sign Jesus did when he came to Galilee from Judea (Jn. 4:46-54).

Jesus' second sign will be the healing of the royal official's son. This took place in the same village in Cana where the first sign at the wedding took place, the very same location where Jesus had turned the water into wine. Jesus is now entering Cana on his return after being gone two days in Judea and Samaria where He interacted with the Samaritan woman at the well during that time. The official had obviously heard about the signs Jesus was performing in Jerusalem and begged Him to heal his son. Jesus first admonishes him saying: "Unless you see signs and wonders you will not believe (Jn. 4:48)."

It is certainly a miracle as the royal official's son is so ill that he is reportedly on the brink of death but what makes this sign more remarkable, is that it takes place at a distance as Jesus tells the man: "Go home, your son will live (Jn. 4:49)."

Jesus, who is the *Logos*, is revealing that His word alone has power because He is The Word. As John had said in describing the *Logos*, in the Prologue in Chapter one: "The Word was God (Jn. 1:2)."

Just as God spoke a word in Genesis and all of creation came into being, just so Jesus speaks a word from a distance and a boy comes from the brink of death back to life. Jesus' word is revelation, but Jesus, The Word, will soon be seen by many as God revealed. Finally, in the healing of the royal official's son, after admonishing the official about "seeing signs," it is noteworthy that seeing had nothing to do with believing. For the royal official, hearing was believing. He had faith in the unseen because of who Jesus is. He would see the evidence of the boy's healing later upon arriving home. This sign also shows that Jesus has control over space and time. Jesus, even at a distance, can send a miracle anytime He wants.

Third Sign-Healing of the Paralyzed Man at the Pool of Bethesda (Jn. 5:1–18)

> After this, there was a feast of the Jews, and Jesus went up to Jerusalem. Now there is in Jerusalem at the Sheep Gate a pool called in Hebrew Bethesda, with five porticoes. In these, lay a large number of ill, blind, lame, and crippled. One man was there who had been ill for thirty-eight years. When Jesus saw him lying there and knew that he had been ill for a long time, he said to him, "Do you want to be well?" The sick man answered him, "Sir, I have no one to put me into the pool when the water is stirred up; while I am on my way, someone else gets down there before me." Jesus said to him, "Rise, take up your mat, and walk." Immediately the man became well, took up his mat, and walked. Now that day was a sabbath. So, the Jews said to the man who was cured, "It is the sabbath, and it is not lawful for you to carry your mat." He answered them, "The man who made me well told me, 'Take up your mat and walk.'" They asked him, "Who is the man who told you, 'Take it up and walk?" The man who was healed did not know who it was, for Jesus had slipped away, since there was a crowd there. After this Jesus found him in the temple area and said to him, "Look, you are well; do not sin any more so that nothing worse may happen to you." The man went and told the Jews that Jesus was the one who had made him well. Therefore, the Jews began to persecute Jesus because he did this on a Sabbath. But Jesus answered them, "My Father is at work until now, so I am at work." For this reason, the Jews tried all the more to kill him, because he not only broke the Sabbath, but he also called God his own Father, making himself equal to God (Jn. 5:1-18).

The third sign, the healing of the paralytic at the pool of Bethesda, called the "Sheep's pool," is intended by John to be much the same as the sixth sign, the healing of the man born blind. With both signs, Jesus acts contrary to the religious leaders, who did not embrace Jesus' healing because it was the sabbath and no healings were allowed. They will also admonish the healed paralytic because it was against rabbinical law to carry your bed-mat on the Sabbath. Here, once again, Jesus' all-powerful word alone will do for the paralyzed man what the waters in the pool could not. Jesus, the Word, will show that His word will suffice to perform the miracle.

The pool, in the shape of a trapezoid, was edged on four sides with porticos and the fifth side transected it at the center dividing it into two pools, each with its own spring. The discovery of the Qumran scrolls identified its exact location as it was referred to as: "The House of the Double Gushers."[2] The pool was said to perform miraculous cures once the waters in it fed by the two natural springs below were stirred up. There were always multitudes of invalids, blind, lame, and paralyzed people who came there seeking to be healed. The poor paralyzed man could not get down into the pool when the springs were active because of the crowd and the fact that he had no one to carry him down into it. The pool remains in the same location to this day and is located near the church of St Anne in Jerusalem. It was a tragedy that the religious leaders disregarded the fact that Jesus' all-powerful word had sufficed to heal the Man after thirty-eight years. To them what was far more important was their unflinching belief in the rabbinical law. They believed that Jesus had broken the Law of Moses by performing this sign on the Sabbath and that he followed this up with what was to them complete blasphemy. By Jesus making the claim that He and His Father are both working still, Jesus is effectively saying that God is His Father, and He is God's Son. This statement is similarly recorded, albeit with different wording, in all three of the synoptic gospels as well: "The Sabbath was made for man, not man for the Sabbath. So, the Son of Man is Lord even of the Sabbath (Mt. 12:1-8, Mk. 2:23-28 and Lk. 6:1-5)."

The rabbinical leaders must have been stopping up their ears with their fingers and making repetitious "la-la" sounds like little children so they would not hear Him any longer as Jesus effectively had said: "I Am the Lord of the Sabbath."

From this point forward, the Jewish religious leaders were now going to seek to kill Jesus for both performing this sign and especially for calling God His Father and Himself, The Lord of the Sabbath, which was showing his equality with God.

Fourth Sign-Feeding of the 5000 (Jn. 6:5–15)

> When Jesus raised his eyes and saw that a large crowd was coming to him, he said to Philip, "Where can we buy enough food for them to eat?" He said this to test him because He Himself knew what he was going to do. Philip answered him, "Two hundred days' wages worth of food would not be enough for each of them to have a little bit." One of his disciples, Andrew, the brother of Simon Peter, said to him, "There is a boy here who has five barley loaves and two fish; but what good are these for so many?" Jesus said, "Have the people recline." Now there was a great deal of grass in that place. So, the men reclined, about five thousand in number. Then Jesus took the loaves, gave thanks, and distributed them to those who were reclining, and as much of the fish as they wanted. When they had had their fill, he said to his disciples, "Gather the fragments left over, so that nothing will be wasted." So, they collected them, and filled twelve wicker baskets with fragments from the five barley loaves that had been more than they could eat. When the people saw the sign he had done, they said, "This is truly the Prophet, the one who is to come into the world." Since Jesus knew that they were going to come and carry him off to make him king, he withdrew again to the mountain alone (Jn. 6:1-15).

This is the only miracle recorded in all four of the canonical Gospels, the synoptics as well as John. Because John the Evangelist composed his Gospel last, there is considerable evidence that he was familiar with the other three, and it seems most definite that he was particularly familiar with Mark's Gospel, even though he did not seek to harmonize with it. This miracle, the feeding of the 5000, had already been developing some significance as a Eucharistic symbol in the early Christian community prior to John writing this Gospel, but he makes explicit what had previously been somewhat implicit in the synoptics. He will give even stronger evidence that this sign has Eucharistic symbolism and significance when he relates the discourse on the "Bread of Life" which will follow in John 6:22–71. By the time Jesus performs this fourth sign, there are multitudes that the miracles have attracted who are following after Him. Although the miracles have attracted a large crowd, they haven't necessarily proven to be a sign of insipient faith to many. Some in the crowd had come to faith in Jesus, many had not, they were just following to see more miracles or signs.

The fourth sign, the feeding of the 5000, is reminiscent of how God fed the Israelites in the desert with manna in the Old Testament Book of Deuteronomy, Chapter 18. Additionally, the barley loaves were the ordinary food of the poor and their use gives rise to the miracle previously performed by the prophet Elisha in the Old Testament Book, 2 Kings 4:42. Thomas Aquinas, in his Biblical commentary on John's Gospel, maintains that the five barley loaves were symbolic of the five Books of Moses under the law and the two fish were symbolic of the Old Testament Book of Psalms and the Books of the Prophets. Aquinas' understanding of this from John's Gospel may have arisen from what was said by Jesus according to Luke's Gospel as Luke records Jesus saying:

> These are my words that I spoke to you while I was still with you, that everything written about me in the law of Moses and in the prophets and psalms must be fulfilled. Then he opened their minds to understand the scriptures (Lk. 24:44-45).

Jesus, giving thanks and breaking the bread to distribute it in verse 11 is also an allusion by John to the Eucharistic sacramentality, symbolism, and significance associated with this miracle. John does not mention all twelve disciples of Jesus as being witnesses to this miracle. However, the twelve baskets of fragments collected which were left from the five barley loaves may have been John's way of giving some indication of that. We really cannot be sure of exactly what was in the mind of John. This sign also shows that there were several in the crowd who were only seeking Jesus for purely material purposes—because He could produce enough food to feed them instantly and further that they found the signs to be intriguing. John is showing here once again that signs do not always lead to true faith in Jesus. Some followers saw only the material food and totally missed the point that Jesus was giving them spiritual food as well as He alone was and is "The Bread of Life." John has Jesus declaring that He is the "Bread of Life" shortly after this sign. Listen for the considerable Eucharistic sacramentality, symbolism, and significance here as Jesus says:

> "I am the bread of life. Your ancestors ate the manna in the desert, but they died; this is the bread that comes down from heaven so that one may eat it and not die. I am the living bread that came down from heaven; whoever eats this bread will live forever; and the bread that I will give is my flesh for the life of the world." The Jews quarreled among themselves, saying, "How can this man give us [his] flesh to eat?" Jesus said to them, "Amen, amen, I say to you, unless you eat the flesh of the Son of Man and drink his blood, you do not have life within you. Whoever eats my flesh and drinks my blood has eternal life, and I will raise him on the last day" (Jn. 6:48-54).

Although not recognizing Jesus as God incarnate, as God in the flesh yet, there are many in the crowd who will believe that Jesus is the Prophet like Moses, as Moses had predicted long ago that God would raise up a future prophet like himself. This was recorded in the Book of Deuteronomy (Dt. 18:15). They did not understand that Jesus isn't just a prophet like Moses, but that He is Lord of the Prophets. In verse 15, following the miracle, Jesus becomes concerned that they wanted to take Him by force and make Him their earthly king. This is recorded somewhat differently in Luke 4 and Matthew 4 where it was the devil who tempted Jesus with an offering of an earthly kingship. Either way, Jesus will have none of it and flees back to the mountain alone.

Finally, what does this miracle recorded by John as well as the other three Gospel writers show us about the nature of Jesus? It shows us that the Lord has tremendous love for his people, He cares for both their material and spiritual needs. Further, it shows us His almighty power, compassion, and providential provision. Through this sign, Jesus is showing the crowd and particularly His disciples and those who have come to place their faith and trust in Him, that He alone is God incarnate and that He can be sufficiency in the midst of any deficiency. Following this miracle, more of the multitude will become believers and place their faith and trust in Jesus; unfortunately, many will not.

Fifth Sign-Walking on Water (Jn. 6:16–21)

> When it was evening, his disciples went down to the sea, embarked in a boat, and went across the sea to Capernaum. It had already grown dark, and Jesus had not yet come to them. The sea was stirred up because a strong wind was blowing. When they had rowed about three or four miles, they saw Jesus walking on the sea and coming near the boat, and they began to be afraid. But he said to them, "It is I. Do not be afraid." They wanted to take Him into the boat, but the boat immediately arrived at the shore to which they were heading (Jn. 6:16-21).

The miracle of Jesus, walking on water is also recorded by Matthew and Mark in their Gospels as well (Mt. 14:22–27; Mk. 6:45–51). The crowd wanted to make Jesus their earthly king. Now Jesus will show that He is so much greater than any temporal, political, or religious ruler. He will show that He is Lord of nature and Lord of the elements. Just as Yahweh controlled the parting of the Red Sea for the Israelites in the Old Testament Book of Exodus Chapter 14, Here John will have Jesus displaying His power over the sea by walking on it which only God can do. Jesus not only has power over the stormy sea, but the wind as well as He quiets it. God alone controls nature and the elements. After all, who can walk on the sea? Who is like God? Have you ever tried this? I know what happens when I try it. . .I can't even float on the sea without going glug, glug, glug like a rock trying to float. In verses 16–19, the disciples are way out to sea and as the wind stirs up; the sea becomes very rough. The disciples become very afraid as they see Jesus walking on the water and coming near to the boat. According to the Jerome Biblical Commentary, verse 20 of John probably represents the chief importance of this event as Jesus tells the fearful disciples in the boat: "It is I" *(ego eimi*, Gk.). This translates to a first-person singular form of the ineffable name of God, "I AM *(YHWH)*," revealed to Moses in the Book of Exodus (Ex. 3:13–14). Once again, John sees a deeper spiritual experience in this simple answer of Jesus as there develops a growing awareness by the disciples of His character and nature.[3] Jesus having said "It is I," to calm the disciples in the boat, is then followed by the most oft-repeated phrase of God recorded in the Bible as the Lord then tells the fainthearted disciples: "Do not be afraid (Jn. 6:20)."

Sixth Sign-Healing of the Man Born Blind (Jn. 9: 1–7)

> As He passed by, He saw a man blind from birth. His disciples asked him, "Rabbi, who sinned, this man or his parents, that he was born blind?" Jesus answered, "Neither he nor his parents sinned; it is so that the works of God

might be made visible through him. We have to do the works of the one who sent me while it is day. Night is coming when no one can work. While I am in the world, I am the light of the world." When He had said this, He spat on the ground and made clay with the saliva, and smeared the clay on his eyes, and said to him, "Go wash in the Pool of Siloam" (which means Sent). So, he went and washed, and came back able to see. (Jn. 9:1-7).

Both this sign and the third sign, the healing of the paralytic, are healing miracles. In some ways these miracles or signs had been predicted by the Prophet Isaiah long before they occurred when Isaiah wrote:

Then the eyes of the blind shall be opened and the ears of the deaf unstopped; then shall the lame man leap like a stag (Is. 35:5-6).

The man had been paralyzed for thirty-eight years and in the case of the blind man, the Gospel says he was blind since birth. Both men waited a long time for the impossible i.e., for someone like Jesus to come along. The question of sin causing the man's blindness is initially dismissed and disregarded by Jesus as He tells the disciples that the man's blindness is more to show God's providential plan at work in the world. Both signs show that Jesus has power over time. Only an eternal God has power over time. These two healing signs wiped out thirty-eight years of sickness for the paralytic and a whole lifetime of blindness for the blind man. Both signs, show that Jesus has compassion for the helpless as both men were significantly reduced physically throughout their lifetimes. However, they were both incapacitated not only in body, but in spirit and hope as well.

With the blind man particularly, John has Jesus also showing the crowd that there is a spiritual dimension of the miracle that many are missing:

Then Jesus said, "I came into this world for judgment, so that those who do not see might see, and those who do see might become blind" (Jn. 9:39).

If you are blind you cannot see, and in order to see, you must have light. Through this miracle, Jesus is essentially saying to the crowd that He is, in fact, the Light of the World, and only God is "the Light of the World." The religious leaders who continually badger, snipe, and chastise Jesus are choosing, in effect, to continue to live in spiritual darkness by opposing not just the necessary "enlightenment" but Jesus, the "Light of the World." Light is useless if one is blind. In this miracle, Jesus will not only give the man his sight which had been missing since birth, but He will give the man the light which he never had as well. John is also showing considerable irony through using this sign. The contrast is stark as this sign will lead to seeing and not blindness for the blind man, both physically and spiritually, as he comes to faith and becomes a disciple of Jesus. On the other hand, this sign will lead many of the religious leaders from seeing the sign to spiritual blindness. Thomas Aquinas will say many years following John's Gospel: "Grace follows nature and as in the natural, so in the spiritual."[4]

The primitive church of the Johannine community saw in this sign much sacramentality and symbolism as John saw the event and the miracle as having considerable baptismal significance. The spittle which Jesus made from His saliva was an anointing in John, and anointing had become part of the Baptismal ritual from the earliest beginnings of the developing church. The baptismal symbolism of this sign was also recorded by both Augustine and Aquinas in each of their commentaries on John's Gospel. In more modern times, it was further highlighted in the Jerome Biblical Commentary on the Bible as well.[5]

Just as the man had been anointed as Jesus "sends" the blind man to the pool of Siloam (the one sent), so also is Jesus the Anointed One (The Christ) and the One sent by the Father. He is anointed and sent to give light not only to the blind man but moreover to the world. As regards the outcome of the miracle of the blind man having received his ability to see, this will occur in both a natural and a spiritual sense. For him seeing becomes only the beginning of belief (Jn. 9:12,17). He will not come to full belief in Jesus until Jesus later seeks him out and finds him. It is then that the blind man will ultimately say: "Lord, I believe (Jn. 9:35-38)." And he will worship Jesus.

The Seventh Sign-The Raising of Lazarus From the Dead (Jn 11: 1–45)

> Now a man was ill, Lazarus from Bethany, the village of Mary and her sister Martha. Mary was the one who had anointed the Lord with perfumed oil and dried his feet with her hair; it was her brother Lazarus who was ill. So, the sisters sent word to him, saying, "Master, the one you love is ill." When Jesus heard this he said, "This illness is not to end in death, but is for the glory of God, that the Son of God may be glorified through it." Now Jesus loved Martha and her sister and Lazarus. So, when he heard that he was ill, he remained for two days in the place where he was. Then after this he said to his disciples, "Let us go back to Judea." The disciples said to him, "Rabbi, the Jews were just trying to stone you, and you want to go back there?" Jesus answered, "Are there not twelve hours in a day? If one walks during the day, he does not stumble, because he sees the light of this world. But if one walks at night, he stumbles, because the light is not in him." He said this, and then told them, "Our friend Lazarus is asleep, but I am going to awaken him." So, the disciples said to him, "Master, if he is asleep, he will be saved." But Jesus was talking about his death, while they thought that he meant ordinary sleep. So, then Jesus said to them clearly,

"Lazarus has died. And I am glad for you that I was not there, that you may believe. Let us go to him." So, Thomas, called Didymus, said to his fellow disciples, "Let us also go to die with him." When Jesus arrived, he found that Lazarus had already been in the tomb for four days. Now Bethany was near Jerusalem, only about two miles away. And many of the Jews had come to Martha and Mary to comfort them about their brother. When Martha heard that Jesus was coming, she went to meet him; but Mary sat at home. Martha said to Jesus, "Lord, if you had been here, my brother would not have died. Even now I know that whatever you ask of God, God will give you." Jesus said to her, "Your brother will rise." Martha said to him, "I know he will rise, in the resurrection on the last day." Jesus told her, "I am the resurrection and the life; whoever believes in me, even if he dies, will live, and everyone who lives and believes in me will never die. Do you believe this?" She said to him, "Yes, Lord. I have come to believe that you are the Messiah, the Son of God, the one who is coming into the world." When she had said this, she went and called her sister Mary secretly, saying, "The teacher is here and is asking for you." As soon as she heard this, she rose quickly and went to him. For Jesus had not yet come into the village but was still where Martha had met him. So, when the Jews who were with her in the house comforting her saw Mary get up quickly and go out, they followed her, presuming that she was going to the tomb to weep there. When Mary came to where Jesus was and saw him, she fell at his feet and said to him, "Lord, if you had been here, my brother would not have died."

When Jesus saw her weeping and the Jews who had come with her weeping, he became perturbed and deeply troubled, and said, "Where have you laid him?" They said to him, "Sir, come and see." And Jesus wept. So, the Jews said, "See how he loved him." But some of them said, "Could not the one who opened the eyes of the blind man have done something so that this man would not have died?" So, Jesus, perturbed again, came to the tomb. It was a cave, and a stone lay across it. Jesus said, "Take away the stone." Martha, the dead man's sister, said to him, "Lord, by now there will be a stench; he has been dead for four days." Jesus said to her, "Did I not tell you that if you believe you will see the glory of God?" So, they took away the stone. And Jesus raised his eyes and said, "Father, I thank you for hearing me. I know that you always hear me; but because of the crowd here I have said this, that they may believe that you sent me." And when he had said this, he cried out in a loud voice, "Lazarus, come out!" The dead man came out, tied hand and foot with burial bands, and his face was wrapped in a cloth. So, Jesus said to them, "Untie him and let him go." (Jn. 11:1–45)

This last of the seven signs is John's certain evidence of Jesus' omnipotent Godly power. To take and paraphrase a line from the play, *Fiddler on the Roof*, this will be the "Miracle of miracles."[6] The account of Lazarus being raised appears only in the Gospel of John. At this point many of the religious leaders are sneering and probably saying something like: "Well, if he opened the eyes of that blind man, you would think that if he truly was the Son of God, he could have kept his good friend Lazarus from dying." Physical death comes to all of us, but there is a spiritual life that can never die. John will have Jesus showing through this sign that He alone has control over that.

The emphasis on glory is one of the most important aspects of this sign. John shows Jesus revealing to the disciples that the purpose of this sign will be to serve the glory of God through this fatal illness and not death. As Jesus says:

> This illness is not unto death; it is for the glory of God, so that the Son of God may be glorified through it (Jn. 11:4).

In verses 11–14, there is another of the several misunderstandings of the words of Jesus in this Gospel as Jesus is intending a deeper, more spiritual meaning about "sleep." Lazarus being asleep has more to it than what the words reveal on the surface. The disciples misunderstand once again, and Jesus tells them plainly: "Lazarus is dead (Jn. 11:14)."

Jesus then relates that he is glad, not that Lazarus died, but that He can increase the faith of the disciples so that: "they may believe (Jn. 11:15)."

Here, the intention of John the Evangelist shows that he is not only concerned about increasing the faith of the disciples with this miracle and his entire Gospel, for that matter, he is concerned with increasing the faith of the Johannine community who had not seen the miracle initially, and secondarily increasing the faith of all believers of all time. John will confirm this fact at the end of his gospel when he writes:

> ...that you may come to believe that Jesus is the Messiah, the Son of God, and that through this belief you may have life in his name (Jn. 20:30).

John is fully aware that many believers at the time he writes the Gospel and throughout time will not have seen any of the seven signs personally and this is his way of affirming their faith and belief in Jesus.

Prior to this miracle, Lazarus is as dead as dead can be. He has been in the ground for four days and must stink a whole lot. Plus, Jews traditionally had maintained the belief that a dead person's soul remained in near proximity to the body for only three days and would then depart. So, this is four days now and supposedly all there is left of poor Lazarus is a whole lot of stink and no soul. It's a common worldwide experience that everybody dies. Even Lazarus once raised by Jesus from the dead will die again another day. So, as Martha relates her faith in a future resurrection of the dead to Jesus (Jn. 11:24), Jesus will advise her that any and all future resurrections are in Him as He says:

I am the resurrection and the life; whoever believes in me, even if he dies, will live, and everyone who lives and believes in me will never die. Do you believe this (Jn. 11: 25-26)?

So, if she and we believe in Jesus and place our trust in Him as our Lord and Savior what is available to us is eternal life now. "Eternal life now" is the offer of Jesus. What is it and do we believe it? There is a theological term for this, and it is something that is threaded throughout John's entire Gospel from start to finish; it's called "Realized Eschatology." Realized Eschatology and "Eternal Life Now" are one and the same thing. They are equivalent to the Kingdom of God, which is coming but is in our midst. It is the Kingdom of God which is somewhere between already and not yet. Remember, John doesn't use the phrase "Kingdom of God" so much. He uses the words, "Eternal Life." So, the "Realized Eschatology" throughout John's Gospel is "Eternal Life Now." [7]

Now, back to the sign of raising Lazarus. Jesus will show his full divinity in raising Lazarus, but first in verse 35, Jesus will show his full humanity as we read: "Jesus wept (Jn. 11:35)."

Fully human is fully divine; fully divine is fully human. Prior to raising Lazarus and more for the crowd's ears than anything else, Jesus will thank the Father. This will also show the crowd that they should not just view Him as a wonder worker in some magic side-show. And then, Jesus will say: "Lazarus; come out! (Jn. 11:43)"

When Lazarus hears Jesus' voice, he emerges from the tomb still wrapped in his burial cloths. John is illustrating here that it is Jesus' voice that raises Lazarus. Jesus is "The *Logos,* The Word of God," and God's word has power, even power over death. John is showing once again with this miracle, that Jesus is not only the revelation of God, but God's glory revealed. The glory is linked not only to the sign, but to faith in Jesus as well. This Book of Signs, and especially this last sign, will serve as a bridge between the *Logos* Prologue and the Book of Glory which will follow. We are told in verse 45, that as a result of the miracle, many of the Jews came to believe in Jesus, but many still did not. John is reaffirming once again, as he had before in his Gospel, that signs or miracles do not always lead to belief in Jesus as God incarnate. Furthermore, after this last of the seven signs, the Sanhedrin will convene to discuss the signs and Jesus' fate as well (Jn. 11:45–47). It is God who controls death and life. In raising Lazarus, John has Jesus showing that He is God. This will also be the sign that will bring on Jesus' "hour." It will point Him in the direction of the cross which will become the penultimate sign for the world. We should note here that in the entire Israelite history, the cross had never been a sign of faith for the Israelites as a people of faith. The seven signs essentially were the beginning of Jesus' glory revealed through the cross and resurrection to come. Soon that glory would become most evident.

Finally, all the seven signs or miracles or works as Jesus called them are important to understanding John's Gospel. They are critical not only to arrive at an understanding that John is presenting Jesus as truly the "Son of God," but also as signposts. These signposts will lead many to faith, not only at the time and setting that this Gospel was written, but today and tomorrow as well. Additionally, they are meant to show that Jesus wishes to share and participate in all aspects of our lives—our joy of weddings, our anguish when sickness or disease overcomes us, our hunger for food, our fear of uncontrolled nature, and often what brings out our greatest fear, the fear of the sorrow of death—not only for ourselves, but even more for those we love. How many times have we all thought that we would rather die ourselves than lose someone we love? The Bible reminds us that love never dies, love is eternal, and only love will be there for us in the end. God is Love and only Jesus' love for us can cast out our greatest fears. Ultimately through His loving power, Jesus can defeat death as well—His, mine and yours (1 Cor. 13; 1 John 4).

NOTES

1. Ibid 2 Chapter 2.
2. http://dss.collections.imj.org.il/
3. Brown, Raymond, ed., Jerome Biblical Commentary, (Englewood Cliffs, NJ, Prentice Hall, 1968), Sec. 63:1–185, pp. 414–466 https://www.worldcat.org/title/new-jerome-biblical-commentary/oclc/657161583
4. Thomas Aquinas, Summa 2nd part no. 109. In the Catholic Encyclopedia. (NY, New York: Robert Appleton Company, 1968). New Advent, Kevin Knight: http://www.newadvent.org/cathen/14333c.htm, Retrieved November 7, 2020.
5. Ibid 3 Chapter 4.
6. Fiddler on the Roof https://www.dailymotion.com/video/x7ncen1
7. Richard McBrien, Catholicism, (NY, NY, Penguin Random House, Crownpublishing.com, 1994).

Chapter 5

The Book of Glory

Glory to Glory

John's Book of Signs ends with Chapter 12. Chapter 13 begins the last week of Jesus' earthly life and is called the Book of Glory. Glory will be the third major theme in John, and he will devote nine chapters of his Gospel (13-20) to discuss the last week of Jesus' human life. Fully one-third, or three of these chapters, will focus on the last 24 hours toward the end of Jesus' biological life on earth.

In the New Testament, the word "glory" has several shades of meaning. For example, the synoptic Gospels, Matthew, Mark, and Luke feature the angel's glorious announcement of Jesus' birth, the glory of the transfiguration, and the Son of Man coming in glory, but John's Gospel develops the themes of glory and glorification in ever so much greater depth. In John, the meaning of the word "glory" will most often signify a manifestation of the divine majesty of Jesus Christ who is the reflection of the Father's glory, filled with grace and truth. The plot of John's Gospel is focused on the "hour" of the glorification of Jesus. This will occur through Jesus' crucifixion and resurrection and will not only work toward his complete Oneness with the glory of God, the Father, but also toward the unification of humankind with God. Mankind, as a creation of God, has an obligation to give glory back to God and Jesus Christ in return through the Holy Spirit who dwells within us. This glory is perceptible only with the eyes of faith and evokes worship and praise but adds nothing to the glory of God, Father, Son, and Holy Spirit. On the other hand, it does allow God's grace and glory to then develop and perfect the likeness of God which exists in the soul of man. God wants each of us to be a perfect and glorious imitation of Christ even though many of us, including myself, continue to feel that we are often no more than just "imperfect saints."

Throughout the Old Testament we read about the "glory of God," which was sometimes manifested in fire or dazzling brightness, too bright for the eye to see. This is what the Israelites called the "Shekinah Glory," the dwelling or settling of the divine presence. In Hebrew, the word used for glory is "*kāḇôḏ.*" The definition of the word is "to be weighty or heavy, and loaded with dignity and power." In the New Testament, *kāḇôḏ* is translated from the Hebrew into the Greek word *"doxa,"* from which we get the English word "doxology," meaning: "a liturgical hymn of praise to God for God's glory," or simply, "the Gloria." Of course, ultimately, God's glory can particularly be seen not just through his signs, but moreover through his actions and deeds. The concept of "Shekinah Glory" is also associated with the concept of the Holy Spirit in Judaism. In John's Gospel, the Book of Glory will reveal that the Incarnate Word will be the new mode of God's presence among His people. Jesus will be the full manifestation of God's divine majesty and power as well as the new temple of God in which God's "Shekinah Glory," will be centered and dwell.[1]

THE GLORIFICATION OF JESUS

Right from the beginning of the Book of Glory as Chapter 13 opens, John announces a turning point in the gospel. To this point, we had learned that Jesus' "hour" had not yet come (Jn. 2:4; 7:30; 8:20). Now comes the declaration that Jesus' hour to depart from the world and go to the Father is at hand (Jn. 13:1). In the account of the crucifixion, Jesus will not be portrayed so much as one who suffers, as in the synoptic Gospels (Mk. 15:25–39). That will not be the focus for John. John will depict Jesus as one who is glorified and exalted. Jesus' hour will soon be upon him which will lead up to Jesus' glory at the cross. The cross especially, along with his subsequent resurrection and ascension are considered as one continuous event and are seen to be the means of Jesus' glorification. Jesus probably knew this from His intimate familiarity with the great "Suffering Servant" passage from the Old Testament Book of the prophet Isaiah that combines the suffering of the servant intimately with the glory. This was described and foretold by the prophet Isaiah in Chapters 52 and 53 long before Jesus of Nazareth ever walked the earth. There is no doubt that Jesus was certainly familiar with the entire Book of this prophet. Recall how he read the Isaiah scroll in the temple (Lk. 4:17–21). Jesus had echoed Isaiah's words in John about being "lifted up" on three different occasions as the manner of his coming glorification and exaltation: "And just as Moses lifted up the serpent in the desert, so must the Son of Man be lifted up (Jn. 3:14)."[2] And: "When you lift up the Son of Man, then you will realize that I AM, and that I do nothing on my own, but I say only what the Father taught me (Jn. 8:28)." And also: "'When I am lifted up from the earth, I will draw everyone to myself.' He said this indicating the kind of death he would die" (Jn. 12:32).

John will also describe in detail this moment of glorification (Jn. 12:16, 23; 13:32; 16:14; 17:1, 5). The Book of Glory, as it opens beginning in Chapter 13 starts with the longest discourse of the entire gospel, where Jesus prepares his disciples for what will soon be His departure (Chs. 13 to 16). This will be followed by Jesus's "high priestly prayer" (Ch.17). Here, Jesus warns the disciples of the world's continued hostility. Jesus promises to send them the Paraclete (Jn. 14:15–16, 26; 15:26; and 16:15). "The Paraclete," translated as "The Advocate" or "the Comforter" is John's special and unique term for Jesus' continued presence with the community in the form of the Holy Spirit. The word Paraclete only appears in the Gospel of John and nowhere else in the entire Bible. We will discuss this term later in a separate sub-theme which is the final chapter of this book.

The closing chapters of the Book of Glory will contain John's account of Jesus' trial, crucifixion, and resurrection. It is interesting to note that The Gospel of John has no narrative of the Lord's Supper, which is different from the synoptic Gospels. In preparing himself and his disciples for his imminent departure and as an illustration of His divine majesty, John will depict Jesus as being in complete control of his mission and his destiny. John will portray Jesus as the victorious savior. Toward the end of the Book of Glory, this will become even more evident as Jesus commends his mother to the Beloved Disciple and ultimately gives up his Spirit (Jn. 19:26–27). The Book of Glory will conclude with an empty tomb story as there are these and a few appearance stories but no descriptions of the actual resurrection itself in any of the Gospels, including John's. There is first the discovery of the empty tomb by the women and disciples (Jn. 20:1–10), then Jesus's appearance to them (Jn. 20:11–18), and the appearance narrative of "Doubting Thomas" (Jn. 20:24–29). The last two verses (Jn. 20:30–31) contain what many biblical scholars believe may have been John's original epilogue. Let's look at why this section (Ch. 13–20) in John's Gospel may have later been termed "The Book of Glory." Leading up to the beginning of the Book of Glory, we find that the first indication of God's glory occurs right at the beginning of John's Gospel in the Prologue. Here Jesus displays the Father's glory in the Son:

> The Word became flesh and made his dwelling among us, and we saw his glory, the glory as of the Father's only Son, full of grace and truth (Jn. 1:14).

The *Logos* Prologue of Chapter 1 will be the last mention of Jesus as the *Logos*, the Eternal Word, in this Gospel. Following the Prologue, John's Gospel will become a testimony to "the Word become flesh" and dwelling among us, Jesus Christ, the Son of Man and Son of God. From then on, Jesus becomes the glory of God revealed. Also following the Prologue, we saw Jesus' glory manifested in His signs, the *(erga,* Gk.) "works." These were displayed in the second theme we discussed, John's Book of Signs (Ch. 2–12). If you will recall, these seven signs were considered as signposts which pointed to who He is—the Son of God. It started with the first sign at the wedding in Cana, when Jesus turned the water into wine. This miraculous act began to reveal His glory: "This, the first of his miraculous signs, Jesus performed at Cana in Galilee. He thus revealed his glory, and his disciples put their faith in him (Jn. 2:11)."

Then also with the last sign, the raising of Lazarus, recall Jesus words when He heard of Lazarus' illness: "When he heard this, Jesus said, 'This sickness will not end in death. No, it is for God's glory so that God's Son may be glorified through it (Jn.11:4)." And then once again, Jesus' words at the tomb of Lazarus: "Did I not tell you that if you believed, you would see the glory of God (Jn.11:40)?"

There is much in John's Gospel which refers to The Father as the source of the Son's Glory as Jesus plainly acknowledges that His glory comes directly from His Father. At the same time, Jesus will also tell the Jewish religious leaders that even though He honors the Father, they dishonor Him:

> I honor my Father and you dishonor me. Yet, I am not seeking glory for myself; but there is one who seeks it, and He is the judge. . .If I glorify myself, my glory means nothing. It is my Father, who glorifies me of whom you say that He is your God (Jn. 8:49–54).

Also, as Jesus talks about his coming hour, which is now close at hand, He will ask the Father to glorify His name. This the Father will acknowledge has already occurred and that He will glorify it again:

> "Father, glorify your name!" Then a voice came from heaven, "I have glorified it, and will glorify it again." The crowd that was there and heard it said it had thundered; others said an angel had spoken to him (Jn.12:28-29).

All the glory of the Father and the Son that John had illustrated in the verses above had occurred well before the actual Book of Glory even begins in Chapter 13. The theme of the glory of the Son will be much more fully developed as the Book of Glory begins. As the Book of Glory begins, Jesus will first discuss how He and the Father will be glorified:

> When he was gone, Jesus said, "Now is the Son of Man glorified and God is glorified in him. If God is glorified in him, God will glorify the Son in himself, and will glorify him at once" (Jn. 13:31–32).

Then John will have Jesus speak of His own glorification, the Father's glory, and the disciples' bearing fruit which will bring glory to God on three more occasions in Chapters 14, 15, and 16 as the Book of Glory continues:

> And I will do whatever you ask in my name, so that the Son may bring glory to the Father (Jn. 14:13).

> This is to my Father's glory, that you bear much fruit, showing yourselves to be my disciples (Jn. 15:8).

> He will glorify me and take what is mine and give it to you (Jn. 16:14).

In the Book of Glory, glory is also brought to Jesus through His disciples as He addresses the Father in prayer in Chapter 17. We see this first as Jesus "lifts up" the disciples in His prayer, offering them up to the Father as having been given to Him and then describing how He is glorified in them. The prayer of Jesus to the Father follows:

> When Jesus had said this, he raised his eyes to heaven and said, "Father, the hour has come. Give glory to your son, so that your son may glorify you, just as you gave him authority over all people so that he may give eternal life to all you gave him. Now this is eternal life, that they should know you, the only true God, and the one whom you sent, Jesus Christ. I glorified you on earth by accomplishing the work that you gave me to do. Now glorify me, Father, with you, with the glory that I had with you before the world began. "I revealed your name to those whom you gave me out of the world. They belonged to you, and you gave them to me, and they have kept your word. Now they know that everything you gave me is from you, because the words you gave to me, I have given to them, and they accepted them and truly understood that I came from you, and they have believed that you sent me. I pray for them. I do not pray for the world but for the ones you have given me, because they are yours, and everything of mine is yours and everything of yours is mine, and I have been glorified in them" (Jn. 17:1–10).

And a little further on in Chapter 17, Jesus will describe his oneness with the Father and the Father's love for the disciples as an extension of their shared mutual love. This oneness will allow the disciples to see the divine manifestation of Jesus' glory:

> And I have given them the glory you gave me, so that they may be one, as we are one, I in them and you in me, that they may be brought to perfection as one, that the world may know that you sent me, and that you loved them even as you loved me. Father, they are your gift to me. I wish that where I am they also may

be with me, that they may see my glory that you gave me, because you loved me before the foundation of the world (Jn. 17:22-24).

Chapter 17:24 is the very last mention of the word "glory" in John. You should be aware that there is a mention after this in Chapter 21:19 using the word "glorify" as Jesus tells Peter how His death is to glorify God. However, this appears in what is called the Epilogue (Ch. 21) which is believed to have really been a second epilogue and a later addition to this Gospel by a disciple of John. We will discuss the Epilogue more in detail as our fourth and final Major Theme in the next Chapter of this book.

Following the final talk of "glory" in Jn. 17:24, shortly thereafter the final hour will be upon Jesus as the crucifixion, resurrection, and ascension occur in Chapters 18, 19, and 20. Even though mention of the word "glory" by John will cease after Ch. 17:24, Jesus through His deeds, not just His words, will manifest the Father's glory, thus bringing a new beginning to the people of the world as the Book of Glory comes to its conclusion with Chapter 20.

St. Augustine maintained that there was a "Golden Thread"[3] that ran through the entire Bible from Old Testament to New Testament because there is always and only one God of the living who is constantly present, speaking and acting in all different times, situations, and historical events. Hence, the risen glory of our Lord Jesus Christ, which John describes in Chapter 20 of his Gospel, is no less than the burning bush of God which was incapable of being consumed that Moses witnessed in The Book of Exodus Ch. 3:1–12. The Book of Glory in John's Gospel (Ch. 13–20) illustrates a continuous manifestation of the "Shekinah Glory" of God found in the Old Testament. Jesus will be the new tabernacle of God's "Shekinah Glory." The plan of God continues to move from glory to glory, as all persons and events are linked together one to another regardless of time or place in history. With this in mind, consider how our beautiful *Battle Hymn of the Republic,* written in 1861, ends so eloquently in giving all glory to God. Each time we sing the words we add nothing to God's glory, however, the glory of God will continue on within us through the Holy Spirit. As the Battle Hymn relates:

Glory, Glory Alleluia! His truth is marching on.[4]

NOTES

1. Ex 3:2, 13:20–22, 19:16–18, 40:34–38; 2 Ch 7:1.
2. Ibid 2 Ch.1.

3. Augustine, Deogratia response, Catechetical Narratio: De Catechizandis Rudebus. Sermon 350A, 1.

4. Howe, Julia Ward, Battle Hymn of the Republic, (NY, NY, Atlantic Monthly, formerly Putnam's Magazine, 1861) Battle Hymn of the Republic. Library of Congress, Washington, DC, 2002. https://www.loc.gov/item/ihas.200000003/

Chapter 6

The Epilogue

Other than The *Logos* Prologue, The Book of Signs, and the Book of Glory, the only other section of John's Gospel which could be considered a major theme is The Epilogue which is the twenty-first and final chapter of this Gospel. It contains an account of the resurrection appearance in Galilee which the text describes as the third time Jesus had appeared to his disciples. Also contained in the Epilogue is the account of the catch of 153 fish, the discussion between the resurrected Jesus and Peter concerning Peter's love for Jesus, and the foretelling of Peter's death and the future life of the beloved disciple who is John, the writer of the Gospel. It seems, Peter had turned around to see John following after he and Jesus. He will then ask Jesus about John's fate in comparison to his own future martyrdom. Jesus' response is a sharp rebuke of Peter (Jn. 21:20–22). He does not use these following words. These are my words which paraphrase what Jesus said to Peter in this Epilogue. But Jesus will essentially be saying to Peter: "Hey Peter; mind your own business, never mind him, and just worry about what I told YOU. You just follow me."

Prior to this Epilogue, John Chapter 20 ends with an epilogue as well, which seems to bring the whole Gospel to a fitting close. For clarification sake, this is often referred to as "The First Epilogue." At the end of Chapter 20, John writes:

> Now Jesus did many other signs in the presence of the disciples, which are not written in this book; but these are written that you may believe that Jesus is the Christ, the Son of God, and that believing you may have life in his name (Jn. 20:30–31).[1]

So, probably the first question we need to ask ourselves is: "Did John the Evangelist intend to write two epilogues?" As we said earlier, the Catholic Church typically uses the Historical-Critical Method in studying the Bible.[2] So, it is generally agreed among most Catholic biblical scholars and theologians that this epilogue called Chapter 21 was not originally part of John's Gospel when he first wrote it. Most Christian biblical scholars agree as well. It was either added by John at a later date, or the more likely scenario is that it was added by a disciple of John or a member of the early Christian church. Either way it seems it was added after the original Gospel was initially written which ended with the first epilogue at the end Chapter 20.

Having a second epilogue appears to be anticlimactic to say the least, but the redactor whoever it was, may have felt that something called an actual epilogue at the end of John's Gospel gave some necessary balance to the prologue at the beginning of the Gospel. Perhaps another scenario might be that the epilogue was added because the disciple in the early church saw some loose ends that needed tying together because of what was going on in the Johannine Community near the end of the first century. There may have been some turmoil or tension which existed between rival groups of Christian believers or some unresolved questions in the community that needed to be addressed. Whatever was surfacing, however, may have tended toward being heretical and needed to be addressed.

There are several other peculiarities in Chapter 21 that make it different than how John, the Beloved Disciple, expressed himself at the location and time and in the language in which he wrote the original Gospel. Particularly, these concern language and stylistic differences. The content is certainly anticlimactic. This is particularly unusual considering not only the previous epilogue at the end of Chapter 20, but also the second epilogue introduces an eighth sign following long after John's book of the seven signs. The Book of Signs was a Major Theme in John Chapters 2–12. Furthermore, in Chapter 20 near its conclusion, Jesus tells the disciples that they are to embark on a mission to evangelize when he says: "As the Father has sent me, even so I send you (Jn. 20:21)."

In Chapter 21, the second epilogue, it does not show us the disciples setting out on the mission of evangelization given by Jesus just prior in Chapter 20, instead the apostles go fishing. Huh? Also, in Chapter 20, the so-called original epilogue, the emphasis is consistently on "believing without seeing," as Jesus tells doubting Thomas just before the chapter's end: "Have you believed because you have seen me? Blessed are those who have not seen and have yet believed (Jn. 20:29)."

As an original ending, this was a word Jesus was speaking not only to Thomas, but also John was speaking to all those throughout time who had no opportunity to see the resurrected Jesus. This should be considered as a word Jesus (through John the Gospel writer), was speaking both to the early Christian church as well as to us. After that was said in Chapter 20, what we find in Chapter 21, the later addition, is just the opposite. The emphasis is then made on both "seeing AND believing."

The fish and bread which the disciples share with the resurrected Jesus for breakfast most likely has some Eucharistic significance. The number of 153 fish caught that appears in Jn. 21:11 also has some symbolic significance as to the universal mission of the disciples. However, there are at least 153 different explanations as to what the symbolism of the number represents. No one of these explanations is spot on and some of the explanations are kind of way out. Therefore, it is probably best to simply say that the number 153 represents an enormous number of large fish that were caught in the net. It may be even more significant perhaps, that the net which held such a great number of large fish was not torn. The net could have signified the early Christian church and the future results of the evangelical commission Jesus had given to His disciples.

The disciples know that it is the resurrected Jesus on the shore, but there is something about His appearance that makes them somewhat uncertain and hesitant. Whether or not the Epilogue was a later addition to the Gospel of John by John himself or a disciple of his, I have always believed that one of the more interesting sections of Chapter 21 occurs in verses 15-17 where Jesus is asking Peter three times: "Peter, do you love me, do you love me, do you love me (Jn. 21:15-17)?"

First, it is believed that Jesus was asking Peter three times because Peter denied him three times when the cock crowed. The threefold confession of Peter is meant to counteract his earlier threefold denial (Jn. 18:17, 25, 27). The three "Do you love me?" questions asked of Peter also include a threefold commission for Peter to be a shepherd. Jesus' response to Peter to "feed my sheep" further indicates the central and key role that Peter would play in the fledgling church. What I think is most interesting of all, however, is that the dialogue is not fully understandable in English. It is far more understandable in the Greek which was the original language used at the time of the writing of John's Gospel. The reason why is because the Greek original language renders the emphasis of the word "love" to be far more pregnant with meaning. In the dialogue between Jesus and Peter, John writes that Jesus used the verb form of "*agape*" in the first two of His three questions: "Peter, do you *agape* me?" Peter answers Jesus with the verb form of "*philos*." The first two times Peter substitutes the Greek word "*philos*" for Jesus' "*agape*" question. We will spend more time on the "love dialogue" between Jesus and Peter when we discuss the Sub-theme of Love present in John's Gospel in Chapter sixteen of this book.

There is an additional important point that the writer of the second epilogue may have wanted to make because of the heresies which had arisen in the church shortly after the original Gospel was written. These heresies surrounded both Jesus' humanity as well as his divinity. Chapter 21 illustrates both the divinity and humanity of Jesus in that Jesus had a resurrected body and that Jesus had a body like our own human body which needed food and drink to nourish it. This post-resurrection appearance is certain evidence of His divinity and his bodily resurrection and the fact He required food and drink is evidence indeed of His humanity. Later, several of the early Christian church councils such as Nicea, Constantinople, Ephesus, and Chalcedon would confirm both Jesus' full divinity and His full humanity in the years which followed between 325 to 451 AD.[3]

Then, in Jn. 21:20–23, as was stated earlier, Peter will first ask Jesus about the beloved disciple John, the more than probable author of the first twenty Chapters of this Gospel. The way Jesus responds seems to indicate the possibility that John had previously died bringing an end to the Apostolic Age[4] as John was the last of the disciples who had been alive. This may have created a problem for the Johannine community and the early Christian church as it was originally believed that Jesus would return before the Apostolic Age ended, and now it may have recently ended with the death of John the Evangelist. Jesus answer will indicate that the Parousia, the second coming of Christ,[5] was still in the future. Here is that dialogue between Jesus and Peter:

> Peter turned and saw the disciple following whom Jesus loved, the one who had also reclined upon his chest during the supper and had said, "Master, who is the one who will betray you?" When Peter saw him, he said to Jesus, "Lord, what about him?" Jesus said to him, "What if I want him to remain until I come? What concern is it of yours? You follow me." So, the word spread among the brothers that that disciple would not die. But Jesus had not told him that he would not die, just "What if I want him to remain until I come? What concern is it of yours?" (Jn. 21:20-23).

Of note here are Jesus words in verse 22 above: "What if I want him to remain until I come (Jn. 21:22)?" This may be seen to provide a transitional linkage between the original ending of the Gospel with Chapter 20 and the now later addition of Chapter 21, the Epilogue. It would now be evident that Jesus would not return before the Apostolic Age had ended. Further evidence that the Parousia, the second coming of Christ, was then seen to be delayed by the early Christian community beyond the Apostolic age can also be found in other parts of the New Testament (i.e., 2nd Peter Ch. 3 and 4).

As the Epilogue moves toward its conclusion, toward the end of Chapter 21, there is even greater evidence that this second epilogue was written by a disciple of John or someone in the early Christian church who was doing some redacting work rather than John the Evangelist. The words seemingly move away from John speaking to us directly in the first person to a combined "WE" (John and a disciple of John) who are then speaking to us:

The Epilogue

It is this disciple who testifies to these things and has written them, and WE know that HIS testimony is true. There are also many other things that Jesus did, but if these were to be described individually, I do not think the whole world would contain the books that would be written (Jn. 21:24).

The fact that John says that he is, "testifying to these things," does not necessarily have to imply that John wrote the words himself with his own hand.

Finally, even though there is considerable evidence verified through the application of the Historical-Critical method that Chapter 21, the Epilogue, was probably a later addition, it appears that the tradition was ultimately derived previously from John the Evangelist directly in an oral tradition. The oral tradition could then have been preserved in written form by some disciple other than the original writer of the previous remainder of the Gospel. The chapter was probably added early on, and not too long after the first 20 chapters were composed. There exists historical evidence that the addition of the Epilogue occurred in written form well before the widespread dissemination of John's Gospel. Furthermore, there is no historical evidence that this Gospel ever circulated without Chapter 21 included. The Epilogue is part of every one of the earliest manuscripts recorded and is today considered an intricate part of John's entire canonical Gospel.

NOTES

1. Ibid Ch 2 no.2.
2. Ibid Ch 2 no. 2a.
3. Wilhelm, Joseph. "General Councils." The Catholic Encyclopedia. Vol. 4. (NY, New York: Robert Appleton Company, 1908). 2 Dec. 2020 . http://www.newadvent.org/cathen/04423f.htm>. Early Church Councils https://www.newadvent.org/cathen/04423f.htm
4. Ibid Ch. 6 no. 3, The Apostolic Age and Fathers https://www.newadvent.org/cathen/01637a.htm
5. Catholic Apologetics, The Parousia, Second Coming of Christ http://www.catholicapologetics.org/ap090500.htm

PART II

The Sub-Themes

Chapter 7

The "I AM" Sayings

In the Book of Genesis and the first few chapters of Exodus, we find God's name recorded as "*El Shaddai*" which can be translated as "God Almighty (Gn. 17:1, 35:110)." God tells Moses and makes him aware that even though He appeared to the patriarchs Abraham, Isaac, and Jacob, establishing His covenant with them, He did not reveal Himself and make Himself known to them by His name (Ex. 6:2-3). However, in the burning bush sequence, which had occurred earlier as recorded in the Book of Exodus (Ex. 3: 13-14), God had previously revealed Himself to Moses. When Moses asked for God's name so he can tell his people who sent him to them, God answers Moses that His name is (YHWH). This is what is called a tetragrammaton, and it is a word-play that preserves the mysterious and transcendent character of the Divine Being even as it reveals something as to the inner meaning of God's name. Because the name is made up of all consonants, it is unpronounceable as it exists in the Hebrew and cannot be translated as is into English.[1]

Ancient Hebrews added vowels to the name, so that God's name would be pronounced as "Yahweh." Many scholars believe that the most proper meaning of the name of God may have been: "He brings into existence whatever exists."[2]

Here is the conversation between God and Moses in the Book of Exodus:

> "But," said Moses to God, "if I go to the Israelites and say to them, 'The God of your ancestors has sent me to you,' and they ask me, 'What is His name?' what do I tell them?" God replied to Moses: "I AM Who I AM." Then He added: "This is what you will tell the Israelites: I AM has sent me to you" (Ex. 3:13-14).[3]

God's name as "I AM" is confirmed six more times in several other of the following Old Testament passages as well. For example:

"God said to Moses, I AM the Lord (Ex. 6:2-3)."

"See now that I, even I AM He (Dt. 32:39)."
"I AM the Lord, your God (Ps. 81:10)."
"I, I AM He (Is. 43:25)."
"I AM He. I AM the first and I AM the last (Is. 48:12)."
"I, I AM He (Is. 51:12)."

"Yahweh," (I AM Who I AM), would be recognized as the proper name of God in the Old Testament. Hence the Jews called it the name by excellence, the great name, the only name, the glorious and terrible name, the ineffable name, the hidden and mysterious name, the unspoken name, the sacred name, the proper name, and most frequently the explicit or the separated name.[4]

To the ancient Israelites-if one knew the name of someone, this implied that you had some power over the being so titled by that name. This is because a name encapsulates a person into a certain defined body and soul and limits them from being any other than that particular person. Moses' question of God's name initiates a reply from God which reaffirms God's transcendent otherness. God would refuse to allow his Holy Name to encapsulate or define him as would the name of any human person. Because God's name is "I AM Who I AM," (*Yahweh*) there is agreement among most Biblical scholars that this name has an etymological connection with the archaic form of the verb "*Hawah*," which means "to be."[5] The name, "Yahweh" would then signify not only God's transcendent otherness, but also his creative and causative power to bring into being whoever and whatever comes into being. "I AM Who I AM" then causes all "to be." Thus, Yahweh alone would be a living God, the God of the living, the God of Abraham, Isaac, and Jacob, and Yahweh alone would be responsible for creating and giving life. As Shakespeare would say long after Moses: "To be or not to be, that is the question."[6]

Furthermore, I should say here that to the ancient Israelites the name of a person was far more pregnant with meaning than it might be today. Currently, names often don't imply much more beyond the name itself. Parents name their children West and Blue, and Ice and Tiffany, which I always thought was a lamp. Well, you know what I mean. However, to the ancient Israelite, the name often captured the very essence of the person. It wasn't simply a moniker. So, "I AM Who I AM," was not only God's personal name as conveyed to Moses, but it was God's essence as well. It is interesting to note further that the word "essence" is from the Latin word *esse* which means "to be."

Beginning in the 6th Century BC, and more frequently from the 3rd Century BC onward, particularly after the destruction of the Temple, God's name was no longer pronounced. Jews ceased to use the name "Yahweh" out of respect and reverence for the divine name. Initially, they used the common Hebrew noun *Elohim* which is translated as "God." Eventually the personal name "Yahweh" became increasingly sacred to Israel and the Hebrew word

Adonai which is translated as "My Lord" began to be used as a substitute for "Yahweh." After the 9th Century AD, the personal name "Yahweh" began to be Latinized across Europe and was mistakenly translated as "Jehovah." It's a long story as to how this came to be the case, but the simple explanation is that after the 9th Century, the term "Jehovah" appeared when Christian scholars took the consonants of "Yahweh" (YHWH) and pronounced it with the vowels of "Adonai (My Lord)." This resulted in the sound *Yahowah* which was a Latinized spelling of "Jehovah." The first recorded use of the name Yahweh as "Jehovah" was believed to have been made in the year 1520. Moving closer to modern times, Christian scholars and theologians in the 19th and 20th Centuries then began to reclaim the original name for the God of Israel, and the name "Yahweh" became God's name once more as it had been at the time of Moses. You've heard it said that "The more things change the more they stay the same." Here is a case in point. It should also be noted that even today many conservative Jews still do not use the proper name "Yahweh" out of reverence for the name and some even write "G_d" instead.[7]

With that as a lot of background, and perhaps even too much detail, we move ahead to the New Testament. We should say first that the name *Yeshua* which is the Hebrew name for Jesus when it is translated into English means "Yahweh Saves" or "I AM Who I AM Who Saves." Now, moving directly into the Gospel of John—he will establish from the beginning of his Gospel, in the *Logos* Prologue, that there is an identification of God (Yahweh) with Jesus of Nazareth. John will describe Jesus as the self-communication and revelation of Yahweh. Jesus is God in human form and not just the revelation of God, but God revealed. Said another way, God (Yahweh) is self-communicated in the very person of Jesus Christ *(The Logos,* Gk.) "The Word." God's only begotten Son becomes flesh and as later described in the New Testament Letter to the Hebrews opening verse: "The Son is the exact representation of the Father's Being (He. 1:1)."

In John's Gospel, the "I Am" statements by Jesus will not function as much as a statement with the noun "I" and the verb "Am." Moreover, they will function in the sense of a name and a complete noun, i.e., "I AM."[8]

With all that having been said—How many times do you think John has Jesus saying: "I AM" in his Gospel? Take a guess. . . its forty-five times. In all the other New Testament books combined, i.e., the other three Gospels plus the Apostle Paul's writings, Jesus says "I AM" only twenty-eight times (with only twelve of those in Matthew, Mark, and Luke). Forty-five times in John! So, to John, Jesus saying "I AM" is an important Sub-theme of his Gospel. There is a total of seven emphatic "I AM" (*ego eimi,* Gk.) statements of the forty-five found in John. With these emphatic statements a metaphorical image completes the "I AM" thought. Almost all of these can be found rooted in the Old Testament as previously being a description of Almighty God "Yahweh." For example:

- The Bread of Life-The Bread from Heaven - see Ex. 16; Nm.11:6–9; Ps. 78:24; Is. 55:1–3; Ne. 9:15; 2 Ma. 2:5–8
- The Light of the World – see Ex. 13:21-22; Is. 42:6-7; Ps. 97:4
- The Good Shepherd – see Ez. 34:1-41; Gn. 48:15; 49:24; Ps 23:1-4; 80:1; 100:3-4; Mi. 7:14
- The Resurrection and The Life – see Dn. 12:2; Ps. 56:13; 2 Ma. 7:1-38
- The Way – see Ex. 33:13; Ps. 25:4; 27:11; 86:11; 119:59; Is. 40:3; 62:10
- The Truth – see 1 Ks. 17:4; Ps. 25:5; 43:3; 86:11; 119:160; Is. 45:19
- The Vine – see Is. 5:1–7; Ps. 80:9–17; Je. 2:21; Ez. 17:5–10

Some of the more noticeable and emphatic New Testament "I AM" statements of Jesus that John records are as follows:

- (The Woman at the Well): "The woman said to him, 'I know that the Messiah is coming, the one called the Anointed; when he comes, he will tell us everything.' Jesus said to her, 'I AM he, the one who is speaking with you.'" (Jn. 4:25–26)
- "I AM the Bread of Life" (Jn. 6:35) and again in (Jn. 6:48)
- "I AM the Bread which came down from heaven" (Jn. 6:41) and similarly in (Jn. 6:51)
- "I AM the Light of the World" (Jn. 8:12)
- "I AM from above and I Am not of this world" (Jn. 8:23)
- "You will die in your sins unless you believe that I AM" (Jn. 8:24) and similarly in (Jn. 8:28)
- "Truly, truly I say to you that before Abraham was, I AM" (Jn. 8:58)
- "I AM the Door" (Jn. 10:7) and again in (Jn. 10:9)
- "I AM the Good Shepard" (Jn 10:11) and again in (Jn. 10:14)
- "I AM the Resurrection and the Life" (Jn. 11:25)
- "When all this takes place, you may come to believe that 'I AM'" (Jn. 13:19)
- "I AM the Way, the Truth, and the Life" (Jn. 14:6)
- "I AM the True Vine" (Jn. 15:1)
- "I AM the True Vine; you are the Branches" (Jn. 15:5)

With all of these preceding "I AM" declarations, and because Jesus is the exact representation of the Father's Being, John the Evangelist through these "I AM" statements on Jesus lips, is establishing in his Gospel the identification of Jesus of Nazareth with God, the Father (*Yahweh*). This identification occurred not only through Jesus' humanity but is also a record from the beginning of John's Gospel of His divine and pre-existent origin in the Godhead.

The divine majesty of the Father is exactly represented in and through the Son. Toward the end of John's Gospel, it will be the third person of the Godhead, the Holy Spirit, whom Jesus will send from the Father. It will be the Holy Spirit who will bear witness to the essential and substantial Oneness of God, Father, Son, and Holy Spirit.

NOTES

1. "YHWH/Yahweh", Encyclopedia Britannica, Jan. 2020. https://www.britannica.com/topic/Yahweh (b) See also "Yahweh," Brown, Raymond, SJ, ed. Jerome Biblical Commentary, (Englewood Cliffs, NJ, Prentice-Hall Publishing, 1968), Sec. 77:11–14.

2. Ibid Ch. 7 no. 1.

3. Ibid Ch. 2 no. 2.

4. "Jehovah (Yahweh)," Maas, Anthony, The Catholic Encyclopedia. Vol. 8. (NY, New York: Robert Appleton Company, 1910). 17 Nov. 2020. http://www.newadvent.org/cathen/08329a.htm

5. Behind the Name, 11/2019, https://www.behindthename.com/name/hawa. See also Harper, Douglas, Etymology Online Dictionary, 2001–2020. https://www.etymonline.com/word/eve

6. Shakespeare, Wm., Hamlet, Act III, Sc I. http://Shakespeare.mit.edu/Hamlet/Hamlet.3.1.html

7. "Jehovah", Encyclopedia Britannica, Sept. 2017, https://www.Britannica.com/topic/Jehovah-2108642 See Also Ibid Ch. 7 no. 1b.

8. Ibid Ch. 7 no.1.

Chapter 8

Faith and Believing

In contrast to the Apostle Paul's New Testament Letters and the synoptic Gospels of Matthew, Mark, and Luke, John never once uses the nouns "faith" or "belief." Why is that do you think? It's because John only uses the verb form of "to believe," and he uses it almost one hundred times in his Gospel. The verb forms used are "to believe" or "believing" (*pisteuo*, Gk.). That bears repeating, the nouns "belief" or "faith" (*pistis*, Gk.) are never used, not even once. He uses the verb "to believe," three times as much as Matthew, Mark, and Luke put together. In fact, in his Gospel, John uses "to believe" or "believing" one-third of all the times they are both stated in the entire Bible.

To John, the implication of believing means that there is deliberate intention as an action to entrust oneself obediently to Jesus with complete confidence. It is "to believe" with the implication of total commitment to the one who is trusted, namely Jesus Christ. Christ is the one who is to be believed. To believe in Christ also means to follow him and to rely on His power. Additionally, believing means that there exists trust in his word and the truth of his revelation when he says:

I AM the Way, the Truth, and the Life (Jn 14:6).[1]

On the other hand, there are times for all of us that we must humbly admit that our believing isn't always exactly like that and we are more like doubting Thomas. It is then we, like Thomas, must say to the Lord:

Lord, I believe, but help my unbelief (Jn. 20:24-31).

Outside of Chapter 21, which we said earlier is considered a later addition to John's Gospel and a second Epilogue[2], if one surveys all the chapters in the original Gospel of John, we see at first glance that there are only two Chapters, Chapter 15 and Chapter 18, that don't contain the verbs "to believe" or "believing." As for Chapter 15, it is a mere technicality, because throughout this chapter as Jesus declares that he is the True Vine, the verb "to remain" (*parameinei,* Gk.) is used by John as a synonym for "to believe." That leaves only one Chapter, Chapter 18, with no mention of the words "to believe" or "believing." If we look at Chapter 18 to try to determine why this is the case for this one lone chapter, we find that it is more a chapter about "unbelieving" than it is about "believing." First, Judas, the Apostle will betray Jesus, thus showing himself not to be a true believer and follower of Jesus. Then the religious officials will arrest him and send Jesus to the high priestly class. Caiaphas, who will interrogate him, does not believe Jesus, and thinks him to be a false Messiah. He sends Jesus on to Pilate for a further trial. Upon Pilate's interrogation of Jesus concerning His kingship, Jesus will say to Pilate: "For this I was born and for this I came into the world, to testify to the truth. Everyone who belongs to the truth listens to my voice (Jn. 18:37)." To which Pilate will respond: "What is truth (Jn. 18:38)?"

It is not fully known whether Pilate asked this question of Jesus, philosophically, rhetorically, playfully, or scornfully. But what is clear is that he walks away after he responds. We can be relatively certain that Pilate will essentially fail to believe that Jesus who is The Way, "The Truth" and the Life, is standing there in front of him. Furthermore, the crowd will not believe that Jesus is the best choice to be set free. They will believe that Barabbas, a robber and revolutionary, rather than Jesus, is a much better choice to be set free (Jn. 18:40). Finally, Peter who earlier was going to "lay down his life" as a testimonial to his believing in Jesus, does a complete about-face and denies Jesus three times (Jn. 18:15–27). Although the word is not used here, Chapter 18 is really a chapter full of "unbelievers."

As far as all the remaining chapters and what they say about believing in Jesus, please see the following citations in John's Gospel: 1:7, 12, 50; 2:11, 22f; 3:12, 15f, 18, 36; 4:21, 39, 41f, 48, 50, 53; 5:24, 38, 44, 46f; 6:29f, 35f, 40, 47, 64, 69; 7:5, 31, 38f, 48; 8:24, 30f, 45f; 9:18, 35f, 38; 10:25f, 37f, 42; 11:15, 25ff, 40, 42, 45, 48; 12:11, 36ff, 42, 44, 46; 13:19; 14:1, 10ff, 29; 15:4–10; 16:9, 27, 30f; 17:8, 20f; 19:35; 20:8, 25, 27, 29, 31.

In terms of the focus of believing, John indicates several different types of believing:

1. To believe that Jesus is the Christ, the Son of God, he who is coming into the world (two times: Jn. 11:27; 20:31).
   a. "She said to him, 'Yes, Lord. I have come to believe that you are the Messiah, the Son of God, the one who is coming into the world (Jn 11:27).'"
   b. "But these are written that you may [come to] believe that Jesus is the Messiah, the Son of God, and that through this belief you may have life in his name (Jn 20:31)."

Faith and Believing 71

2. To believe that the Father sent Jesus (three times: Jn. 11:42; 17:8,21).
   a. "I know that you always hear me; but because of the crowd here I have said this, that they may believe that you sent me (Jn. 11:42)."
   b. "The words you gave to me I have given to them, they accepted them and truly understood that I came from you, and they have believed that you sent me (Jn. 17:8)."
   c. "...so that they may all be one, as you, Father, are in me and I in you, that they also may be in us, that the world may believe that you sent me (Jn. 17:21)."
3. To believe that "Jesus is God" through the expression "I AM" (two times: Jn. 8:24; 13:19).
   a. "That is why I told you that you will die in your sins. For if you do not believe that I AM, you will die in your sins (Jn 8:24)."
   b. "From now on I am telling you before it happens, so that when it happens you may believe that I AM (Jn 13:19)."
4. To believe that Jesus comes from God, the Father (two times: Jn. 16:27, 30).
   a. "For the Father himself loves you, because you have loved me and have come to believe that I came from God (Jn 16:27)."
   b. "Now we realize that you know everything and that you do not need to have anyone question you. Because of this we believe that you came from God (Jn 16:30)."
5. To believe that Jesus is in the Father and the Father is in Jesus (two times: Jn. 14:10,11).
   a. "Do you not believe that I am in the Father and the Father is in me? The words that I speak to you I do not speak on my own. The Father who dwells in me is doing his works (Jn 14:10)."
   b. "Believe me that I am in the Father and the Father is in me, or else, believe because of the works themselves (Jn 14:11)."
6. To believe in the scriptures (one time: Jn. 2:22).
   a. "when he was raised from the dead, his disciples remembered that he had said this, and they came to believe the scripture and the word Jesus had spoken (Jn 2:22)."
7. To believe in Jesus' word (three times: Jn. 2:22b; 4:50; 5:47b)
   a. "...they came to believe the scripture and the word Jesus had spoken (Jn. 2:22b)."
   b. "Jesus said to him, 'You may go; your son will live.' The man believed what Jesus said to him and left (Jn 4:50)."
   c. "But if you do not believe his (Moses) writings, how will you believe my words (Jn 5:47b)?"
8. To believe in the works of Jesus (one time: Jn. 10:38).

a. "If I perform them, even if you do not believe me, believe the works, so that you may realize and understand that the Father is in me and I am in the Father (Jn. 10:38)."
9. To believe in Jesus and believe in never dying (one time: Jn. 11:26).
    a. "Everyone who lives and believes in me will never die. Do you believe this (Jn. 11:26)?"

One of the reasons John does not use the noun form for "belief" or "faith" is to show that there is dynamic action in "believing." The verb forms "to believe" or "believing" are actions one does, and belief and faith should not be simply an object one possesses as a matter of intellectual assent. Neither should we simply be content with a credo as a set of principles to which we adhere or see as a guide for our actions. To John, the believer is either moving forward in believing or falling back; because it is dynamic, there is no standing still. There is always dynamic and active movement. Recall that the word for "spirit" in the Greek is "*dynamis*" from which we get our English word "dynamic." To John, if one is "believing" then the Spirit (the *Dynamis,* Gk.) of God is actively working in the person. For example, John has Jesus saying: "Truly-truly, I tell you, whoever believes has eternal life (Jn. 6:47)." Also, Jesus proclaims: "Whoever believes in me believes not only in me but also in the one who sent me, and whoever sees me sees the one who sent me (Jn. 12:44-45)."

In this passage Jesus proclaims that believing in him also empowers one to believe in the one who sent him, The Father. In addressing doubting Thomas toward the end of this Gospel, John will have Jesus saying to Thomas: "Blessed are those who have not seen and yet have come to believe (Jn. 20:29)." Believing is an assurance of what we hope for and a conviction of things we cannot see as we are promised in the Letter to the Hebrews. Therefore, our faith and hope must rest primarily in the unseen. What is seen is temporary; what is unseen is eternal. When faith becomes seen, hope is then realized, so that in the end all that will remain is love. Love is eternal. There are certain synonyms that John uses for "believing" or "to believe" as well. They include "knowing or to know," "seeing or to see," "receiving or to receive," "accepting or to accept," and "remaining or to remain." When used by John these synonyms will convey that one is, in fact, "believing." In the end, the result for believing in Jesus Christ as God, can lead a person toward a number of different ending points in this Gospel:

....to become children of God (Jn. 1:12)
....to become children of light (Jn. 12:36)
....to have eternal life (Jn. 3: 12-16)
....to pass from death to life (Jn. 5:24)

....to live and never die (Jn. 11:25-26)
....to never be hungry or thirsty (Jn. 6:35)
....to have living water (Jn. 7:38)
....to receive the spirit (Jn. 7:39)
....to be Jesus' disciple (Jn. 8:31)
....to be Jesus' friend (Jn. 15:14-15)
....to see the glory of God (Jn. 11:40)

To sum up, "faith" to John is the virtue of "believing" even if we do not understand or even actually see. Faith is never a noun and always a verb to show that it is dynamic and active—not static-nor an object of intellectual acceptance-nor a credo to which we hold fast. If John were going to use a description of "faith" in his Gospel as a synonym for "believing," John wouldn't actually use the word "faith." He would say something like "faithing" and that would render faith as a verb to show that it is active and dynamically moving either forward or backward. Obviously, there is no such word as "faithing" so, this is hypothetical as the word is never used by John.

I don't think there are any known statistics to support the statement I'm about to make, but I've heard it said several times that more souls throughout the ages have come "to believe" that Jesus Christ is their Lord and Savior through the Gospel of John than through any other book of the Bible. The only supporting statistic I can verify for you is that I am one of them. A long time ago a Christian friend shared his believing with me by giving me a copy of the Gospel of John and suggesting that I just read it prayerfully. The Holy Spirit given to me in Baptism stirred in me as I read, and I came to believe in God's word as being living and active in the Sacred Scriptures. All I did was merely read John's Gospel and truly interiorize God's word for the first time. The Holy Spirit of God did all the rest.

Finally, the act of "believing" in John's Gospel should lead those who come "to believe" in Jesus to eternal life. The conclusion to the Gospel of John appears at the end of the original epilogue in Chapter 20 and it ends on a note of believing. It is a reaffirmation of the first promise of eternal life made by Jesus to those who come to believe in Him which appeared early on in Jn 3:14–15. Here is the original ending that is seen as a conclusion to the Gospel of John:

> Now Jesus did many other signs in the presence of his disciples that are not written in this book. But these are written that you may come TO BELIEVE that Jesus is the Messiah, the Son of God, and that BELIEVING you may have life in his name (Jn. 20: 30-31).[3]

NOTES

1. Ibid, Ch. 2 no. 2.
2. See Ch. 6, The Epilogue.
3. "Faith and Believing in Johannine Thought," Brown, Raymond, SJ, ed., Jerome Biblical Commentary, (Englewood Cliffs, NJ, Prentice-Hall, Publishing, 1968), Sec 80:35–38.

Chapter 9

Knowing and Unknowing

One of the foremost Catholic theologians of our time has been the late Karl Rahner, a German Jesuit scholar. Rahner's theology has been called by many a "theological anthropology" because it begins with the study of the human person in relation to their knowledge of God. In his theological writings concerning the knowing of God, one of the several important points that he has made that concerns man's knowledge of God is as follows:

> Matter and spirit are one because they have their origin in God. Matter is always becoming, striving for spiritual existence. This striving reaches fulfillment in the human being, which is self-conscious matter able to know and love, and love has primacy to knowledge...Knowing God is far more important than knowing about God.[1]

To John the Evangelist, "knowing God" is strictly and solely through the person, words, and works of Jesus Christ. John's knowing was rooted in his personal knowing and loving of Jesus and not based solely on any certainty of mind or intellectual assent. In his First Epistle, John tells us:

> Beloved, let us love one another, because love is of God; everyone who loves is begotten by God and knows God. Whoever is without love does not know God, for God is love (1 Jn. 4:7)[2]

To John, the way for us to know God is by loving one another because "God Is Love." If we don't have love, then we don't know God. In this life, however, it will remain as our reality at all times that even in our knowing God our knowledge will be incomplete because God's reality is rooted in transcendence and profound mystery. Therefore, our unknowing of God will always be greater than our knowing God.[3] This is the reason why the great spiritual classic of the fourteenth century, "*Cloud of Unknowing*," written anonymously, has told us: "Do not seek God through knowledge, but through simple love."[4]

In this, the church age, it is through the Paraclete, the Holy Spirit within the church and in the believer, that "knowing God" through Jesus Christ can occur. The Spirit interprets Christ's teachings and then imparts Christ's life in love. The Spirit thus unites the believer to God, who is love, empowering the believer to "know God." John tells us about the Spirit (Paraclete) and knowing and loving Jesus as God as follows in his Gospel:

> If you love me, you will keep my commandments. And I will ask the Father, and he will give you another Advocate to be with you always, the Spirit of truth, which the world cannot accept, because it neither sees nor knows it. But you know it, because it remains with you, and will be in you (Jn. 14:15-17).

Others can only become aware that any believer "knows God" through the manifestation of the Holy Spirit in the believer who will produce the Fruit of the Spirit. The Holy Spirit will first manifest itself in love, but also includes joy, peace, patience, kindness, goodness, faithfulness, gentleness, and self-control (Gal. 5:22). The Bible tells us that these are the fruit of the Spirit. In his Gospel, John tells us that good fruit is evidence that the branch on the vine is good, and the believer knows God and has a relationship with God. Bad fruit might be evidence that the branch might be bad and there is a question as to how well the believer "knows God (Jn. 15:1-17)."

In the Gospel of John, there are a few forms of the verb for "knowing," which are two different Greek words John uses: There is the Greek verb *ginosko*, which implies a kind of knowing that includes the way of acquiring information; however, John uses it in a way that especially implies an experiential knowledge and not merely the accumulation of informational facts. The basic meaning of *ginosko* in John, is to know by experience. This type of knowing, however, has a number of nuances including to get to know, to come to understand, and to have intimate relations with another. With knowledge gained by experience there can be an active relationship between the one who knows and the person known. This is a far superior form of knowing by experience and is what every Christian should desire as their personal experience regarding their relationship with the Person of Christ. Here the verb refers to knowledge which is an experience which includes spiritual knowledge which occurs through the action and manifestation of the Holy Spirit in the believer. John gives some examples of this form of knowing as Jesus tells us:

> If you continue in my word, you are truly my disciples, and you will know the truth, and the truth will make you free (Jn. 8:31-32).

And in a more intimate form of knowing in Chapter 10:14–15 on the Good Shepard as Jesus says:

> I Am the Good Shepard; I know my own and my own know me, as the Father knows me, and I know the Father (Jn. 10:14-15).

This particular verb, *ginosko,* with all of its nuanced meaning is used by John fifty-seven times in his Gospel.

There is another Greek verb for knowing which is *eido.* This is used by John more frequently. In fact, he uses *eido* eighty-four times in this Gospel. This particular verb, implies "knowing by perception." It involves a more intuitive or insightful kind of knowing. It is more mystical and spiritual. It is most often used by John as a kind of knowing which believers are given by and through the Holy Spirit. *Eido,* suggests a fullness of knowing, as opposed to *ginosko* being a kind of progressive or gradual form of knowing. Let's look at an example of where John uses *eido* in Jn. 13:1–11 where the verb *eido* is used four times as the verb for "knowing":

> It was just before the Passover Festival. Jesus KNEW that the hour had come for him to leave this world and go to the Father. Having loved his own who were in the world, he loved them to the end. The evening meal was in progress, and the devil had already prompted Judas, the son of Simon Iscariot, to betray Jesus. Jesus KNEW that the Father had put all things under his power, and that he had come from God and was returning to God, so he got up from the meal, took off his outer clothing, and wrapped a towel around his waist. After that, he poured water into a basin and began to wash his disciples' feet, drying them with the towel that was wrapped around him.
>
> He came to Simon Peter, who said to him, "Lord, are you going to wash my feet?" Jesus replied, "You do not KNOW now what I am doing, but later you will understand." "No," said Peter, "you shall never wash my feet." Jesus answered, "Unless I wash you, you have no part with me." "Then, Lord," Simon Peter replied, "not just my feet but my hands and my head as well!" Jesus answered, "Those who have had a bath need only to wash their feet; their whole body is clean. And you are clean, though not every one of you." For he KNEW who was going to betray him, and that was why he said not everyone was clean (Jn. 13:1-11).

When it comes to "knowing God," John will often illustrate this by combining "knowing" with "not knowing." Here are three examples:

> Then they asked him, "Where is your father?" "You do not KNOW me or my Father," Jesus replied. "If you KNEW me, you would KNOW my Father also" (Jn. 8:19).

> If you love me, keep my commands. And I will ask the Father, and he will give you another advocate to help you and be with you forever—the Spirit of truth. The world cannot accept him because it neither sees him nor KNOWS him. But you KNOW him, for he lives with you and will be in you (Jn. 14:15–17).
>
> Righteous Father, though the world does not KNOW you, I KNOW you, and they KNOW that you have sent me. I have made you KNOWN to them, and will continue to make you KNOWN in order that the love you have for me may be in them and that I myself may be in them (Jn. 17:25-26).

In all three of the above examples we can see how John had combined KNOWING with NOT KNOWING. For us as Catholics and Christians, knowing God cannot be separated from knowing Jesus through the action of the Holy Spirit, nor can knowing Jesus be separated from the church which is the deposit of the Holy Spirit sent by Jesus from the Father. The Jesus we know should be confirmed and affirmed in Christian community with other believers and other "knowers" of Jesus. Even knowing Jesus implies whether we might know Jesus as a casual acquaintance, a close friend, or as our beloved. The Jesus each of us knows can be different based on our life's experience and knowing Jesus should be a relationship that can grow stronger and closer just like any relationship we have. Jesus is not just another historical figure from the past like Aristotle or Napoleon or George Washington. They are all dead, but Jesus Christ is alive and present to us today in and through the Holy Spirit. It is possible for us to "know God" today and find Jesus alive in John's Gospel. The scriptures tell us this in the Letter to the Hebrews: "Indeed, the word of God is living and effective, sharper than any two-edged sword, penetrating even between soul and spirit, joints and marrow, and able to discern reflections and thoughts of the heart (Hb. 4:12)."

Through the grace of God and the working of the Holy Spirit in us, God's word in John's Gospel or any other book of the Bible can come alive in the church and in us as believers. This allows for the reception of God's self-communication today in both Word and Sacrament. As this occurs, we can know Jesus not only as one who lived long ago and was written about by John 2000 years ago, but through reading and interiorizing the living word in the Gospel of John as Jesus truly becomes alive as an active, present, and living word within us.

GNOSTICISM

One final note in relation to knowing God through knowing Jesus in the Holy Spirit: In both his Gospel and the Johannine letters 1, 2, and 3, John is addressing not only the believers in the early Christian community and believers throughout all time, but many heretical false teachers, false prophets, and anti-Christian sects as well. In the second century AD, shortly after the Gospel of John was written, there arose an organized heretical movement in the Christian church called "Gnosticism." Gnosticism actually had its beginnings in the pre-Christian era. It confused the kind of "knowing" that John as well as the Apostle Paul and others were speaking and writing about, with a very different and corrupt form of knowing. The Gnostics believed in and spread a very different anti-Christian message that involved having some secret and private knowledge or "gnosis" in order to find salvation. This was unlike orthodox Christianity which emphasized that the Christian with the indwelling of the Holy Spirit through grace and an active faith in Jesus Christ, might find salvation. This contrasted with Gnosticism which believed that the soul attains its proper end by obedience of mind and the possession of secret knowledge of the mysteries of the universe. This was different indeed as Gnostics were "people who supposedly knew," but what they failed to know was essentially what the Gospel writer John told us—that it is God who saves us through Jesus Christ having sent the Holy Spirit to indwell in us. No secret or private knowledge we possess, no matter how profound, is going to save us. Knowledge cannot save, Jesus saves.[5]

The Christian refutation of the Gnostics can be seen threaded early on throughout both John's Gospel and the Johannine letters, 1 John, 2 John, and 3 John, as well as the Apostle Paul's many letters. Through John's emphasis on many dualistic themes in his Gospel such as light and darkness, life and death, knowing and unknowing, etc., he will take on the dualism which had such a heavy emphasis in Gnosticism and meet the many gnostic false teachers head on. One Gnostic in particular John was addressing in his Gospel and his three letters was Cerinthus, a contemporary of The Evangelist John, who was a member of a heretical Christian sect in Ephesus.[6] Following the Evangelist John and the Apostle Paul, several of the early church Fathers refuted the Gnostics as heretics in their writings as well.

Some examples of these early Christian Fathers who refuted Gnosticism were the apologies of Justin Martyr, Tertullian, and the letters of St Irenaeus. St. Irenaeus was a disciple of St. Polycarp who was a direct disciple of St. John. It would become the Letters of St. Irenaeus and those of Tertullian that would specifically tell us later in the second century of the adversarial struggles for the souls of early Christians in the first century through the

Gospel and letters of St John.[7] John's Gospel and his writings with their many dualistic themes contained his refutations of the dualistic writings inherent in the Gnostic heresies of his time and the writings of Cerinthus in particular. Organized Gnosticism eventually died out after a time, but like cockroaches making a comeback, it is difficult to stamp out the Gnostics completely. Many splinter groups lasted as organized pseudo-Christian heretical sects long after St John died and up until the fifth century. These Gnostic sects after they die out for a time, however, suddenly appear again in different cultic forms, even in modernity. Scientologists and Christian Scientists might be a few examples of modern-day forms of neo-Gnosticism, as well as several of the so-called "New Age" cultic religions.[8] Because John's Gospel is a "living word," today's Gnostics and what they believe can be similarly refuted with a living word from John's Gospel, just as they were back in the first century when John lived and wrote.

NOTES

1. Get Real, M. Hickey, (Lanham, MD, Univ. Press, 2017)—See also Enc. Of Theology, K. Rahner, ed. (NY, NY, Seabury Press, 2012).

2. Ibid Ch. 2 no. 2.

3. Karl Rahner, Internet Encyclopedia of Philosophy, https://iep.utm.edu/rahner/

4. Anonymous, Cloud of Unknowing; Univ of Rochester.; Robbins Lib., Dig., P. Gallagher, Ed;326–328; 423f; 999–1000f. https://www.library.rochester.edu/spaces/robbins

5. Gnosticism, New Advent Encyclopedia, https://www.newadvent.org/cathen/06592a.htm. Vol. 6, (NY, NY, Robert Appleton Co.,1909), Dec. 5, 2020.

6. Ibid, Ch.9, no.5, see also Cerinthus, Catholic Encyclopedia, https://www.newadvent.org/cathen/03539a.htm

7. Fathers of the Church, Catholic Encyclopedia, https://www.newadvent.org/cathen/06001a.htm

8. Encyclopedia Britannica, New Age Movement, April 2017, https://www.britannica.com/topic/New-Age-movement

Chapter 10

Light and Darkness

Throughout the Old Testament, light was used as a symbol or metaphor for life and goodness (Pr. 4: 18-22). Light was also intimately associated with the presence of God (Ex. 3:1-17; Ps. 104:1-2; 139:11-12) as well as the Word of God (Ps. 119:105). The Greek word for light used in John's Gospel is *"phos"* from which we get our English word "phosphorus" which has the attribute of glowing in the dark.[1]

The theme of "light and darkness" is a significant sub-theme in the Gospel of John. John discusses the theme of light nine times in his Gospel beginning with a reference to Jesus being the light of life and the light of the human race in the *Logos* Prologue of Chapter 1. One of the properties of light in a natural sense is that it is an agent to create life. It should be noted that "light" in John's Gospel is never defined in terms of a righteous kind of light, like "shining a light on our sins," but more in terms of life, i.e., Jesus' life. We are told here as well that Jesus' "life" is light. Thus, the light which He has brought into the world connects with the life that is in Him, and results in us having His life within us through the Holy Spirit. Jesus' light and life, we are also told in the *Logos* Prologue to this Gospel, empowers us to become children of God, born not of blood or the will of the flesh or man, but of God. To illustrate this with a natural metaphor, John is essentially saying that Jesus is not only the sun (s-u-n) containing light and life within itself as the source of light and life, but Jesus is also the rays of the sun, imparting, illuminating, penetrating, shining, and shedding its light to create life in all the darkness. Believing in Jesus is similar to a sunny day and not a dark night where you can stumble and fall. In contrast with the light, the parallel figure of darkness can represent uncertainty and ignorance, but the main usage of darkness by John is to illustrate separation from God. We can choose separation from God and live in darkness because we have a free will; however, nothing can ever separate us from the love of God. Even when we might willfully choose darkness over light, God never withdraws his love for us in Christ Jesus.

We find the first mention of Jesus' life being the true light of the human race in the *Logos* Prologue of Chapter 1:

> ...through him was life, and this life was the light of the human race. The light shines in the darkness, and the darkness has not overcome it (Jn. 1: 4–5).[2]

Immediately after that we are told that John had come to testify to the light and that the true light was coming into the world to enlighten us so that we might believe. A little further on in the Gospel we find that even when the light had come into the world that people still preferred darkness to the light because of their wicked deeds. Only those who live in truth will come toward the light:

> A man named John was sent from God. He came for testimony, to testify to the light, so that all might believe through him. He was not the light but came to testify to the light. The true light, which enlightens everyone, was coming into the world (Jn. 1:6-8).

> And this is the verdict, that the light came into the world, but people preferred darkness to light, because their works were evil. For everyone who does wicked things hates the light and does not come toward the light, so that his works might not be exposed. But whoever lives the truth comes to the light, so that his works may be clearly seen as done in God (Jn. 3:19-21).

Added to the core symbol of light in this Gospel are some subordinate symbols used by John the Evangelist which describe light in many subtle and nuanced ways. For example, fires, torches, lanterns, day as opposed to night, etc. Additionally, Jesus will also use the subordinate symbol of a burning and shining lamp to describe John the Baptist and his mission and how people were content to rejoice in his light for a while until Jesus came as the true light (Jn. 5:35–36). Furthermore, Jesus will describe himself not only as the true light but as the light of the world:

> Jesus spoke to them again, saying, "I am the light of the world. Whoever follows me will not walk in darkness but will have the light of life" (Jn. 8:12).

Light in the natural sense means that which illuminates and makes things visible. Without light entering the eye, seeing is impossible. Blindness can also imply a lack of moral and spiritual light which enlightens us in the mind, soul, and spirit. John will often use light and darkness in this latter way with having a spiritual connotation as he describes Jesus as "the light of the world."³

Light as a theme in this Gospel is first, a metaphor. Metaphors are conceptual language and are understood to be more than simply a substitution of one word for another. Saying Jesus is "The Light" does more than simply provide a different word to name God. Metaphors are a way that our mind works to conceive one thing in terms of another. People think about a thing by making connections to something else they know. John knows that his hearers and readers of his Gospel know what light is. He wants them metaphorically to make that leap which will allow them to know who Jesus is as the light of the world. Perhaps the best illustration of how John uses the theme of light and darkness occurs in Chapter 9 of this Gospel with the story of the man born blind. This is a key chapter that John will use to highlight the theme of light and darkness as well as seeing and blindness. He uses Jesus' cure of the man born blind in a physical sense as a metaphor to illustrate spiritual blindness and the darkness that many walk in.[4] The narrative in a spiritual sense will contrast Jesus' light with the Jewish religious leaders' blindness:

The Man Born Blind

> As he passed by he saw a man blind from birth. His disciples asked him, "Rabbi, who sinned, this man or his parents, that he was born blind?" Jesus answered, "Neither he nor his parents sinned; it is so that the works of God might be made visible through him. We have to do the works of the one who sent me while it is day. Night is coming when no one can work. While I am in the world, I am the light of the world." When he had said this, he spat on the ground and made clay with the saliva, and smeared the clay on his eyes, and said to him, "Go wash in the Pool of Siloam" (which means Sent). So, he went and washed, and came back able to see. His neighbors and those who had seen him earlier as a beggar said, "Isn't this the one who used to sit and beg?" Some said, "It is," but others said, "No, he just looks like him." He said, "I am." So, they said to him, "[So] how were your eyes opened?" He replied, "The man called Jesus made clay and anointed my eyes and told me, 'Go to Siloam and wash.' So, I went there and washed and was able to see." And they said to him, "Where is he?" He said, "I don't know." They brought the one who was once blind to the Pharisees. Now Jesus had made clay and opened his eyes on a sabbath. So, then the Pharisees also asked him how he was able to see. He said to them, "He put clay on my eyes, and I washed, and now I can see." So, some of the Pharisees said, "This man is not from God, because he does not keep the sabbath." [But] others said, "How can a sinful man do such signs?" And there was a division among them. So, they said to the blind man again, "What do you have to say about him, since he opened your eyes?" He said, "He is a prophet." Now, the Jews did not believe

that he had been blind and gained his sight until they summoned the parents of the one who had gained his sight. They asked them, "Is this your son, who you say was born blind? How does he now see?" His parents answered and said, "We know that this is our son and that he was born blind. We do not know how he sees now, nor do we know who opened his eyes. Ask him, he is of age; he can speak for himself." His parents said this because they were afraid of the Jews, for the Jews had already agreed that if anyone acknowledged him as the Messiah, he would be expelled from the synagogue. For this reason his parents said, "He is of age; question him." So, a second time they called the man who had been blind and said to him, "Give God the praise! We know that this man is a sinner." He replied, "If he is a sinner, I do not know. One thing I do know is that I was blind and now I see." So, they said to him, "What did he do to you? How did he open your eyes?" He answered them, "I told you already and you did not listen. Why do you want to hear it again? Do you want to become his disciples, too?" They ridiculed him and said, "You are that man's disciple; we are disciples of Moses! We know that God spoke to Moses, but we do not know where this one is from." The man answered and said to them, "This is what is so amazing, that you do not know where he is from, yet he opened my eyes. We know that God does not listen to sinners, but if one is devout and does his will, he listens to him. It is unheard of that anyone ever opened the eyes of a person born blind. If this man were not from God, he would not be able to do anything." They answered and said to him, "You were born totally in sin, and are you trying to teach us?" Then they threw him out. When Jesus heard that they had thrown him out, he found him and said, "Do you believe in the Son of Man?" He answered and said, "Who is he, sir, that I may believe in him?" Jesus said to him, "You have seen him and the one speaking with you is he." He said, "I do believe, Lord," and he worshiped him. Then Jesus said, "I came into this world for judgment, so that those who do not see might see, and those who do see might become blind." Some of the Pharisees who were with him heard this and said to him, "Surely we are not also blind, are we?" Jesus said to them, "If you were blind, you would have no sin; but now you are saying, 'We see,' so your sin remains" (Jn. 9:1-41).

It should be further stated that the epitome of darkness John refers to throughout his Gospel is more the darkness of rejecting God's Son, Jesus and God's message of the offer of eternal life, rather than the darkness of being unenlightened or committing sin. As light will lead to life; ultimately, darkness will only lead to death. Jesus will warn his disciples and believers:

> If one walks during the day, he does not stumble, because he sees the light of this world. . . . The light will be with you only for a little longer, walk while you have the light, lest the darkness overtake you; he who walks in the darkness doesn't know where he goes... I came into the world as light, so that everyone who believes in me might not remain in darkness (Jn 11:9; 12:35, 46).

This warning is very prophetic. In fact, it is interesting to note that the theme of light is not going to be discussed by John any longer after Chapter 12 ends and the Book of Glory begins in Chapter 13 and runs through to Chapter 20. Why do you think that is the case? Why isn't John going to use the light metaphor any longer now after Chapter 12? It's because Chapter 12 marks the end of Jesus' public ministry! The nation of Israel had a chance to receive Jesus, the Light of the world. But they didn't for the most part, and John is illustrating by their refusal the intentional omission of the theme of light in the final eight chapters of the Book of Glory. It is both because of their refusal and the ensuing crucifixion that the light was removed from the world and thus from the remainder of his Gospel as well. Like much in John's Gospel there is a dualism expressed within the sub-theme of Light and Darkness as there is with several other of John's sub-themes, such as Knowing and Unknowing, Seeing and Blindness, Life and Death, etc. There is more of this dualism expressed in John's Gospel than in any other book of the Bible.

This was probably done to illustrate that throughout history there has been a continuous conflict going on dualistically between good and evil. The realm of light is the world above, from where Jesus descended into His humanity. The realm of darkness is this world, the world below, where Jesus has come from above to bring the light because he is: "The Light of the World (Jn. 8:12)."

Although John will contrast light and darkness as symbolic of the contrast between good and evil, he also has a secondary motive in his comparing and contrasting light and darkness. To John, darkness is also symbolic of the old covenant under the law compared to light being symbolic of the new covenant under Jesus Christ who offers us life in the Spirit. The light and the life, who is Jesus, now shines even brighter following the incarnation and the resurrection through the presence of the Holy Spirit. John was an eyewitness to this, and his Gospel is written with this light and life now shining for him in the rear-view mirror.

Finally, another one of the properties of light is that it reveals things and allows them to grow.[5] Throughout his Gospel, John is in no small way, using the physical theme of light which is something natural to suggest a greater theme of spiritual illumination. This suggests that God through the Holy Spirit can create within us that illumination which will allow us to grow and to see and know Jesus as He is revealed to us both as the Light of the world and as the Living God who can offer us life. Following this, we are left with the choice of either deciding to walk in his light and choose life or deciding to continue to walk in darkness which can only lead to death.

NOTES

1. "Phosphorus," Douglas Harper, Etymology Online Dictionary, 2001, https://www.etymonline.com/search?q=phosphorus
2. Ibid, Ch.2, no. 2.
3. Lusby, Franklin MD, 2018, NIH, National Library of Medicine, Medline Plus, https://medlineplus.gov/ency/anatomyvideos/000109.htm
4. "Metaphor." Merriam-Webster.com Dictionary, Merriam-Webster, https://www.merriam-webster.com/dictionary/metaphor. Accessed 19 Nov. 2020.
5. Stark, Glenn, Encyclopedia Britannica, October 29, 2020, https://www.britannica.com/science/light, November 19, 2020.

Chapter 11

Seeing and Blindness

In John's Gospel, "seeing" is associated closely with light. As was discussed in the previous chapter, seeing is impossible without light.[1] If there is blindness, seeing is impossible even with the presence of light as the light is of no benefit to someone who cannot see. John will present both seeing and blindness in the natural sense as well as being implied in a spiritual sense in his Gospel.

In the Old Testament, God cannot be seen because His radiance is too much for human eyes. God is then revealed through His glory by being present and hidden in a pillar of cloud or in a fire (Ex. 13:21; 24:17). In Jesus, who is God incarnate, God is not only present but seen. Seeing is a verb and a sub-theme, which is central to John's Gospel. In the study of John's vocabulary, Catholic scholar, Fr. Raymond Brown, cites the verb "seeing" as used in several various forms in the Gospel a total of one hundred and fourteen times.[2] Not only is this usage far more than any of the other Gospels, but far more than any other part of the Bible. To some in John's Gospel, seeing is a cause for believing; however, the greater audience that John is addressing primarily are those who have neither seen Jesus in the Johannine community of his day as well as those like us today who will only read or hear his Gospel long after Jesus' crucifixion and resurrection.

Chapter 9 where Jesus heals the man born blind and interacts with the religious leaders is a key event John uses to describe not only light and darkness, but also both seeing and blindness. In this chapter there are certain individuals like the blind man who cannot see in the natural sense and the light is useless to him. He will come to see both in a natural sense as Jesus opens his eyes to the light as well as come to see the light in a spiritual sense. He will gradually come to believing in Jesus as God incarnate. There are others, like many of the religious leaders, who see in a natural sense, but do not see with the eyes of their heart and are blind in a spiritual sense. They either do not see or will not see. The blind man first "sees" Jesus as 'the man called Jesus,' as he says:

"The man called Jesus made clay and anointed my eyes and said to me go to Siloam and wash, so I went and washed and received my sight (Jn. 9:11)."[3]

In verse 17, the blind man sees Jesus as more than simply a man as he relates: "He is a prophet (Jn. 9:17)."

A little later the blind man sees Jesus as being: "from God (Jn. 9:33)."
And finally, the blind man will then gradually come to seeing along with believing in Jesus as first the Son of Man and then his Lord, as he worships him. Here are those verses at the close of Chapter 9:

> When Jesus heard that they had thrown him out, he found him and said, "Do you believe in the Son of Man?" He answered and said, "Who is he, sir, that I may believe in him?" Jesus said to him, "You have seen him and the one speaking with you is he." He said, "I do believe, Lord," and he worshiped him (Jn. 9:35-38).

This stands in stark contrast to many of the Jews and their religious leaders who were totally unaware of their spiritual blindness. Their hunger for power and influence and their controlling positions as interpreters and enforcers of the Mosaic laws and the temple codes were like horse blinders on the eyes of their hearts. They didn't "see" that there was someone greater than the temple and their adherence to the law as well. They were blind to the fact that this is: "The Light of the world" right in front of their eyes. They were in fact, truly blind as they were "seeing" Jesus as "not from God, not keeping the Sabbath, sinful, and this one." Here are those sequences in Chapter 9:

a. Not from God-Not keeping the Sabbath: "So, some of the Pharisees said, 'This man is not from God, because he does not keep the sabbath.' Others said, 'How can a sinful man do such signs?' And there was a division among them (Jn. 9:16)."
b. A sinner: "So, a second time they called the man who had been blind and said to him, 'Give God the praise! We know that this man is a sinner (Jn. 9:24).'"
c. This one: "They ridiculed him and said, 'You are that man's disciple; we are disciples of Moses! We know that God spoke to Moses, but we do not know where this one is from (Jn. 9:28-29).'"

Finally, their implicit blindness is revealed as explicit blindness in the dialogue between the religious leaders and Jesus as their spiritual blindness is unmasked as they respond by saying:

a. We see: "Then Jesus said, 'I came into this world for judgment, so that those who do not see might see, and those who do see might become blind.'" Some of the Pharisees who were with him heard this and said to him, "Surely we are not also blind, are we?" Jesus said to them, "If you were blind, you would have no sin; but now you are saying, 'We see,' so your sin remains (Jn. 9: 39-41)."

Another example of spiritual blindness on the part of the Jews and their religious leaders can be found with Nicodemus in John 3:1–10. Here is the dialogue between Jesus and Nicodemus illustrating the spiritual blindness of Nicodemus:

> Now there was a Pharisee named Nicodemus, a ruler of the Jews. He came to Jesus at night and said to him, "Rabbi, we know that you are a teacher who has come from God, for no one can do these signs that you are doing unless God is with him." Jesus answered and said to him, "Amen, amen, I say to you, no one can see the Kingdom of God without being born from above." Nicodemus said to him, "How can a person once grown old be born again? Surely, he cannot reenter his mother's womb and be born again, can he?" Jesus answered, "Amen, amen, I say to you, no one can enter the kingdom of God without being born of water and Spirit. What is born of flesh is flesh and what is born of spirit is spirit. Do not be amazed that I told you, 'You must be born from above.' The wind blows where it wills, and you can hear the sound it makes, but you do not know where it comes from or where it goes; so it is with everyone who is born of the Spirit." Nicodemus answered and said to him, "How can this happen?" Jesus answered and said to him, "You are the teacher of Israel and you do not understand this?" (Jn 3:1-10).

Toward the end of John's Gospel there is evidence that the spiritual blindness of Nicodemus was lifted and that he began seeing Jesus as the Son of God with the eyes of his heart. In Chapter 19, we find that Nicodemus had become a disciple and a secret believer because of the Jews along with Joseph of Arimathea:

> After this, Joseph of Arimathea, secretly a disciple of Jesus for fear of the Jews, asked Pilate if he could remove the body of Jesus. And Pilate permitted it. So, he came and took his body. Nicodemus, the one who had first come to him at night, also came bringing a mixture of myrrh and aloes weighing about one hundred pounds (Jn. 19:38-39).

Threaded throughout this Gospel there are others interspersed who "come and see" and gradually begin to believe. For example, early in Chapter 1 following the *Logos* Prologue, John will use Nathaniel as an illustration of seeing and believing:

Philip found Nathanael and told him, "We have found the one about whom Moses wrote in the law, and the prophets, Jesus, son of Joseph, from Nazareth." But Nathanael said to him, "Can anything good come from Nazareth?" Philip said to him, "Come and see." Jesus saw Nathanael coming toward him and said of him, "Here is a true Israelite. There is no duplicity in him." Nathanael said to him, "How do you know me?" Jesus answered and said to him, "Before Philip called you, I saw you under the fig tree." Nathanael answered him, "Rabbi, you are the Son of God; you are the King of Israel." Jesus answered and said to him, "Do you believe because I told you that I saw you under the fig tree? You will see greater things than this." And he said to him, "Amen, amen, I say to you, you will see the sky opened and the angels of God ascending and descending on the Son of Man" (Jn. 1:45-51).

John also uses Martha as an example in Chapter 11:22–27 as at the end of her dialogue with Jesus she will bear witness to him as she testifies to Jesus being the resurrection and the life, the Messiah, and the Son of God just before he will raise her brother Lazarus from the dead: "Yes, Lord. I have come to believe that you are the Messiah, the Son of God, the one who is coming into the world (Jn. 11:27)."

And lastly, perhaps one of the best examples of "gradually coming to see" and ultimately believing in Jesus is the woman at the well in Chapter 4. Here are some of the Samaritan woman's "gradually coming to see" responses:

"Sir, give me this (living) water (Jn. 4:15)."
"Sir, I perceive you are a prophet (Jn. 4:19)."
"I know that Messiah is coming who is called The Christ (Jn. 4:25)."

Then in verse 29, as the Samaritan woman runs to tell all the city folk to "come and see," she wonders if Jesus might be the Christ:

Come see a man who told me all that I ever did. Can this be The Christ (Jn. 4:29)?

Finally, in verse 42 along with many of the Samaritans of that city, we see how she bears witness to Jesus that is far different from the time she initially interacted with Jesus and saw him as only a prophet: "We know that this is indeed the Savior of the world (Jn. 4:42)."

In conclusion, this Gospel had been written toward the end of the first century AD. By that time many years had elapsed, and as a consequence very few of the original eyewitnesses of Jesus' resurrection were still alive. Unlike John the Evangelist, almost all of John's readers (including us) were born after the resurrection. Most of these people were excluded from the possibility of seeing the risen Lord. They had to rely on the testimony of the apostolic witnesses preserved by John and the early Christian church who had actually seen the risen Lord.[4] As we read John's Gospel today, we must depend heavily upon that "apostolic seeing" and the testimony of the early church Fathers who bear witness for us in the Christian church today. The believers in the community John is addressing with his Gospel (including us today), had no opportunity to visibly see the earthly Jesus. Toward the conclusion of his Gospel, John will address this as Jesus tells doubting Thomas:

> Jesus said to him, "Have you come to believe because you have seen me? Blessed are those who have not seen and have believed" (Jn. 20:29).

It is our believing in Jesus Christ through the grace of God that empowers the Holy Spirit to allow us today to "come and see" Jesus as a living Word in John's Gospel. For the time being, this "seeing," will only occur through the eyes of our heart as our faith continues to remain in the unseen.

NOTES

1. Ibid Ch. 10, no. 3.
2. Ibid Ch. 4, no. 3.
3. Ibid Ch. 2, no. 2.
4. "The Apostolic Fathers/ The Apostolic Age," Peterson, John Bertram, The Catholic Encyclopedia. Vol. 1. (New York, NY: Robert Appleton Company, 1907). 5 Dec. 2020 http://www.newadvent.org/cathen/01637a.htm

Chapter 12

Ascent and Descent

John's Dualism

Have you noticed how many of the sub-themes we've been discussing are dualistic? Do you see the dualism between ascent and descent, believing and unbelieving, knowing and unknowing, light and darkness, seeing and blindness? With these dualistic themes, what John is really alluding to is the ultimate dualism which is beyond even life and death. It is the age-old battle between good and evil since the beginning of time. The word "Gospel" literally means "Good news." John as well as Matthew, Mark and Luke are each in their own way, describing Jesus as "The Good News." It is no accident that only John has Jesus referring to himself as the "Good Shepard (Jn.10:11)." The Gospels of Matthew and Mark both discuss Jesus in terms of being a Shepard of the lost sheep (Mt. 2:6, 9:36, 25:32, 26:31; Mk. 6:34, 14:27), but only in John is Jesus referred to as the "Good Shepard (Jn. 10:11)." The dualism John is presenting in his Gospel is not just passive opposition but more an illustration of continuous warfare. Death is battling against life, darkness against light, seeing against blindness, and these are ultimately representative of good battling against evil.[1] This will be even more evident later when John writes the Book of Revelation also called the Apocalypse while imprisoned on the Isle of Patmos. It is filled with even more dualism than his Gospel.

All four Gospels, Matthew, Mark, Luke, and John contain much dualism. The Gospel of John, however, contains a very distinctive and different way that it is presented. The dualism in the Synoptic Gospels is primarily horizontal; it is a contrast between two ages – this age and the age to come. We also know from the Apostle Paul's use of language that even when he uses the words "this world," this is also the equivalent of Paul saying, "this age." Its most often the same type of dualism used in the synoptic Gospels; it is usually horizontal. Whereas the dualism in John is primarily vertical: a contrast between two worlds—the world above and this world below. The ascending and descending of Christ will occur vertically between these two worlds. That is why the ascent and descent theme is so critically important to John's Gospel.

ASCENDING AND DESCENDING

Almost right at the beginning of this Gospel, shortly after the Prologue on the *Logos*, John will be giving us some indication that ascent and descent will be one of his sub-themes as John the Baptist first tells us:

> I saw the Spirit descend as a dove from heaven and it remained on him. I myself did not know him; but he who sent me to baptize with water said to me, He on whom you see the Spirit descend and remain, this is He who baptizes with the Holy Spirit. And I have seen and borne witness that this is the Son of God (Jn. 1:32-33).[2]

Not long after that, John has Jesus saying to Nathaniel after he was called along with Phillip: "Truly, truly, I tell you, you will see heaven open and the angels of God ascending and descending on the Son of Man (Jn. 1:51)."

The allusion John is making here is to the Jacob's ladder incident which occurred during Jacob's dream as outlined in The Book of Genesis Ch. 28:12–13. While on his way to Padanaram in Mesopotamia, Jacob stopped at Bethel and lay down to rest. He began to dream and during his dream, he saw a stairway which rested on the ground with its top reaching to the heavens and the angels of God ascending and descending on it. The Lord stood next to Jacob in the dream telling him that the land he was lying on would be given to him and his numerous descendants in whom all the families of the earth would find blessing.

Shortly after Jesus speaks with Nathaniel about the angels of God ascending and descending on the Son of Man, Jesus will attempt to instruct Nicodemus on the necessity of a new birth from above. He will initially give this answer to an inquiring Nicodemus who wants to know about being "born again." Jesus will answer:

> Jesus answered and said to him, "Amen, amen, I say to you, no one can see the kingdom of God without being born from above...Do not be amazed that I told you, 'You must be born from above.'" (Jn. 3:3,7).

Nicodemus shows his lack of spiritual knowledge in his interaction with Jesus. The Greek adverb *anōthen,* used in the text can mean both "above" and "again." Jesus' answer means "from above" but Nicodemus misunderstands it as "again." Jesus will attempt to clarify this misunderstanding on the part of Nicodemus later in verses 13 and 31. He will further instruct Nicodemus through an allusion to his ascending and descending as Jesus tells Nicodemus:

> If I have told you earthly things and you do not believe, how can you believe if I tell you heavenly things? No one has ascended into heaven but he who descended from heaven, the Son of man...The one who comes from above is above all. The one who is of the earth is earthly and speaks of earthly things. But the one who comes from heaven [is above all] (Jn. 3:13, 31).

Following two of the signs in the Book of Signs—the feeding of the 5000 and Jesus walking on water which are the fourth and fifth signs, John will record the Bread of Life Discourse given by Jesus. During this discourse, Jesus will make it clear to the disciples, the crowd, and all who are listening that he has descended from heaven. This occurred, not to fulfill his own will but to fulfill the Father's will, and to complete the mission that he received from the Father to raise believers on the last day and offer them eternal life (Jn. 6:38). When his mission from the Father is fulfilled, Jesus must ascend to heaven from whence he had descended (Jn. 6:62). In this section of John's Gospel, Jesus will tell all who are listening a total of eight different times in the Bread of Life discourse: "I Am the Bread of Life...the Living Bread who descended from heaven (Jn. 6:33-58)."

But the disciples as well as many of the Jews and especially the religious leaders will find this statement by Jesus either hard to believe, not understandable or unacceptable that he could have descended from heaven. How is that possible, they will ask? They will claim to know Jesus as the son of Joseph and to know his father and mother, therefore descending from heaven is an impossibility to them. They will refuse to believe in Jesus and reject his offer of eternal life. Shortly thereafter, Jesus will specifically address the murmuring of the shocked disciples by telling them: "Does this shock you? What if you were to see the Son of Man ascending to where he was before (Jn. 6:61-62)?"

As a result, many of his disciples were unbelieving and some returned to their former way of life while no longer accompanying him. Meanwhile, arguing between the religious leaders, the scribes, and pharisees will continue. Jesus, for His part, becomes increasingly aware that they are now trying to kill him. The crowd will continue its murmuring over his words about descending from heaven and ascending back to heaven once again. Divisions in the crowd are beginning to form as many will believe and begin to follow Jesus, but many will not simply disbelieve, they will now criticize, ridicule, and try to arrest Him. The religious leaders will confront Jesus once again after He first embarrasses them about throwing the first stone at the woman caught in adultery. Jesus then declares that He is: "the Light of the World (Jn. 8:12)."

When they accuse Jesus of testifying on his own behalf, he corrects them and then responds:

> You belong to what is below, I belong to what is above. You belong to this world, but I do not belong to this world (Jn. 8:23).

THE ASCENSION

The Ascension can be described as the ascending of Christ from this world and his return into the presence of the Father in the world above (heaven) from which he descended. Jesus, having sent the Holy Spirit from the Father after his glorification, will continue to be present to us. The glorification, resurrection, ascension, and sending of the Spirit are thus all seen as one event. Jesus had fulfilled the promise that he had made to the disciples at the Last Supper of continuing His presence with us. John wants the community of believers then and throughout all time to be aware that Jesus is still among us through the Spirit of Jesus whom He sent from the Father and who lives within us and remains with us. Jesus tells us:

> I will ask the Father, and he will give you another Advocate to be with you always, the Spirit of truth, which the world cannot accept, because it neither sees nor knows it. But you know it, because it remains with you, and will be in you. I will not leave you orphans; I will come to you. In a little while the world will no longer see me, but you will see me, because I live and you will live. On that day you will realize that I am in my Father and you are in me and I in you (Jn. 14:16-20).

As was stated previously, the Gospel of John contained two earlier references to the ascension which are given to us in Jesus' own words:

> No one has ascended into heaven but he who descended from heaven, the son of man (Jn. 3:13).

> What if you (the disciples) were to see the son of man ascending where he was before (Jn. 6:62)?

There remains one final reference to the ascension in Jesus' own words that he relates to Mary Magdalene after his resurrection and that appears almost at the end of John's Gospel as Jesus says:

Stop holding on to me, for I have not yet ascended to the Father. But go to my brothers and tell them, "I am going to my Father and your Father, to my God and your God." Mary of Magdala went and announced to the disciples, "I have seen the Lord," and what he told her (Jn. 20:17-18).

Several centuries after John's Gospel was written, these references to the Ascension will be formed into a creedal statement of Christian belief in what we call "the Apostles' Creed"[3] in which we recite: "He ascended into heaven and is seated at the right hand of God the Father almighty."

In the first and second reference to the Ascension in John, Chapters 3 and 6, Jesus is claiming to be "one like a Son of Man" which is taken from the Old Testament apocalyptic Book of Daniel (Dn. 7:13–14). The last of the references to the Ascension that is given to Mary Magdalene has mystified Biblical scholars and commentators for centuries. One is left to wonder, why should Mary Magdalene be prohibited from touching the risen but not yet ascended Christ (Jn. 20:17–18), while (doubting) Thomas is shortly thereafter invited to do so in Jn. 20:24–29? Does the answer lie in the fact that the two instances in John's Gospel are only separated by a few verses? Might the separation between the two instances imply, however, that they did not necessarily occur one right after the other as the verses might indicate from their being in close proximity? Could it be that Jesus ascended right after talking to Mary Magdalene? Is His appearance to Mary a pre-Ascension one and His appearance to Thomas the first of many Post-Ascension appearances? One could hold such a view if seeing the Ascension after forty days described in Acts 1:1–11 by Luke as simply a termination of Jesus' earthly appearances after the Ascension and more as an introduction to our being baptized in the Holy Spirit with the conferral of the Spirit upon the early Christian church. This church remains to this day as the deposit of the Holy Spirit sent by Jesus from the Father as "another Paraclete." In this church, Jesus is present to us in both Word and Sacrament and very much alive after having ascended.

The Ascension itself should not be seen as the temporary absence of Jesus from our world as Jesus is always present with us through the Holy Spirit. Jesus and Heaven are synonymous; Heaven is the person of Jesus as Heaven is in Him. To the Gospel writer John, the term "eternal life" is often used as his equivalent to the Kingdom of Heaven or the Kingdom of God.[4] When we raise our hearts to heaven, we enter into the eternal life of Jesus Christ in the now moment. This life can be the beginning of our eternal life in heaven and a foretaste of our own ascension into it. Through the Holy Spirit our destiny will always be intimately bound with the destiny of Jesus Christ who has already ascended.

NOTES

1. Ibid Ch. 4, no. 3.
2. Ibid Ch. 2 no. 2.
3. "Apostles' Creed," Thurston, Herbert, The Catholic Encyclopedia. Vol. 1. (New York: Robert Appleton Company, 1907). 20 Nov. 2020 http://www.newadvent.org/cathen/01629a.htm
4. "Life Eternal," Brown, Raymond, ed., Jerome Biblical Commentary, Englewood Cliffs, NJ, Prentice Hall, 1968), 63:1–185, pp. 414–466, see also "Ascension," JBC, Sec. 63:170–179; 78:159.

Chapter 13

Life and Death

The word "life" appears almost fifty times in the Gospel of John. You should be aware however, that there are multiple Greek words used in the bible such as *Zoe, Psychi, and Bios* that translate into the word "life.". The translation of *Bios* implies "biological life," and *psychi* when it is used, always implies that it is "soul life." John will never use the word *bios* even once and almost never uses the Greek word *psychi*. The one word for "life" that the Gospel writer John will use much more than any and almost exclusively, is the Greek word *zoe*. Here the Greek word refers to the uncreated, eternal life of God, the divine life uniquely possessed by the Eternal God. John has such an emphasis on "eternal life" in his Gospel that he will use that term *zoe* five times more than Matthew, Mark, and Luke.

One of the major reasons John had for writing his Gospel is to provoke faith in Jesus, which will lead to eternal life. He is writing both to call unbelievers to faith in Jesus Christ and to provide confidence for those believers who are struggling with their faith. At the time John is writing, many false teachers have arisen in the Christian community who are denying Jesus' divinity or his true humanity. There are also many unbelievers who have rejected Jesus' claim to be the Messiah and the self-communication and self-revelation of God. John first demonstrates that Jesus confirmed through his teaching and his "signs" (which Jesus referred to as His "works") that he truly came from the Father. He came from heaven, the world above, to this world to bring eternal life to all who believe in Him.

One of the things that is distinctive in John that you may have noticed already is that John doesn't say too much about the Kingdom of God or the Kingdom of Heaven that is talked about extensively in the synoptic Gospels and is a major theme in Matthew, Mark, and Luke. In fact, John only mentions the words "Kingdom of God" twice. Why do you think that is? It is because to John, "eternal life" is the Kingdom of God. It is a present reality. Eternal life is in the now moment and is John's unique way of describing the Kingdom which is in our midst and realized in Jesus Christ. It is God's offer extended to us as adopted children of God and a sharing in His eternal life. One of the reasons that John will use the term "eternal life" instead of "Kingdom of God," as is used by the synoptic Gospel writers, is to draw a distinction between what they saw as "ahead" and appearing with Jesus at the second coming, as contrasted with John seeing eternal life as "above" and present in the now moment. It is where Jesus descended from heaven and will ascend back to the Father.[1]

As far as eternal life, we don't know too much about that because we neither know too much about God's life or for that matter, what eternity is exactly. Probably one thing we can say with certainty about eternal life though is that it is God's life which he tells us through Jesus that we can have a share in. Eternal life then is life in eternity with God. Beyond that, we don't really know what God's eternal life is exactly like. We just have to trust that the life which Jesus promised us—eternal life—will fill us with love, joy, and blessedness. So, even though we can't say too much about eternity, which is God's life, there are a few things God tells us about Himself that extend metaphorically to our grasp of eternity. For example, because God tells us that He is the Alpha and the Omega, the Beginning and the End, that says one thing which describes eternity metaphorically, without saying too much more with assuredness. That is: "eternity is a circle." A circle has no beginning and no end. So, as it was sung in the play, *The Lion King,* "it's the circle of life." Hakuna Matata![2]

Let's continue with our discussion of "eternal life" in John's Gospel...The *Logos* Prologue in this Gospel began with the words: "In the beginning was the Word, and the Word was with God, and the Word was God (Jn. 1:1)."

So, God was, is, and always will be. God is in the present moment, the "now" moment, but God is eternal as well. Just as we can't picture God in our imagination, similarly, we cannot picture God's life in eternity in our imagination. Every attempt we make to envision eternity results merely in some lengthened view of imaginary time. The point is that time, of course, is essentially different from eternity. Unlike eternity, we as human persons can grasp some concept of time. We know that the concept of time usually implies six elemental considerations, those being succession, continuity, divisibility, movement, measurability, and irreversibility. In time, the future can never be completely detached from the past and the present since it comes from the past and through the present. This connection would be impossible if the present did not come from the past and was not open to the future, which is still outstanding, though not yet fully known or realized. Yesterday and reality lose their meaning if today has no tomorrow. The past is that which is gone; however, it exists because of the present which can be seen as that future which is arriving now AND that future which is still outstanding.

Without a future which is still outstanding there can be no concept of time as we know it.

However, anytime we try to make a leap from that understanding of time to an understanding of eternity, all we can imagine is some concept of lengthened time running on and on and on, which is time everlasting but not eternity. It will only be in some future moment in time as we are incorporated fully into the Godhead that all present and past moments will eventually be understood. Right now, how can we understand eternity if we are not even able to understand the beginning of time which took place in the past where Jesus Christ was, but we were not.

Second, how are we able to understand the end of any and all future moments of time which we haven't as yet experienced; even though Jesus has? The point is that we are dependent upon Jesus for our sharing of eternal life, and what we will eventually know as the past, present, and future. Third, even talking about the past, present, and future says more about time than it says anything at all about eternity. The incarnation of Jesus Christ is the high point at which eternity and time intersect. The cross of Christ is the bridge from here to eternity for each and every one of us.[3]

As each of us passes through our human death, we will enter new life in Christ. It is only then that the Lord will lead us into a new life which leads on into an eternity without beginning or end. This eternal life will be representative of our new life in Christ because we know that when we see Him, we will be like Him as God is the Alpha and the Omega, the beginning and the end. In eternity, time will no longer be a limitation for us as we experience an eternal opportunity. For us now, as death approaches, time is continually running out, in eternity it will be continually opening up. What kind of an experience that will be, we have no clue, but in his first epistle John tells us:

> Beloved, we are now children of God, and what we will be has not yet been revealed. We know that when Christ appears, we will be like Him, for we will see Him as He is (1Jn. 3:2).

Even though we have not had an experience of eternal life, God has, and there are some things God has revealed which tell us about God's life. In the 6th century, the Catholic lay philosopher, Boethius, tried to give us a theological definition of eternity. Eternity was defined by Boethius as: "possession, without succession and perfect, of interminable life."[4]

This definition, which applies to eternity properly and thus applies to God, implies four things that eternity probably is. It is:

- a life,
- without beginning or end,

- without succession,
- of the most perfect kind.

By definition this implies that God not only "is," essentially or exists, but that God "lives." John tells us in the *Logos* Prologue: "In him was life, and that life was the light of all mankind (Jn. 1:4)."

One of the problems with this, however, is that the notion of life, like all notions whether abstract or spiritual, is when applied to God, only an analogy. God does not live precisely as anything else with which we are familiar, nor does God even exist as anything else exists. As Creator, God is uncreated, and God's reality is a transcendent reality. In other words, God's reality is over and above any reality that we have seen, experienced, or comprehended. We cannot simply project our realty onto God because we are created beings and God is uncreated. God is, was, and always will be. God's life is not like ours. Our notion of life or essence and existence is derived from creatures we know in which life implies change. Existence is something which is added to our essence or "isness," thus it involves composition. In God there can be no composition, change, or imperfection of any kind, but all is pure act or pure being. God is "infinitely perfect" in God's eternity.

So, in many ways we are back to square one and still do not know too much about God or "eternal life," a life which we only know is God's life. That is at least a beginning even though it's not "in the beginning." God tells us that He is without beginning or end. Unlike events which take place in time, in eternity events do not follow a sequential pattern, they are entire or whole. We could pose the question, of course, "What was God doing before time began?" But that would be utter nonsense and an absurdity because any "before" involves time and not eternity. Even St Augustine saw that question as a theological absurdity back in the early centuries A.D.[5] Without an Eternal One, who is Creator, you cannot have creation, hence you cannot have created life. All created things come into existence at a point in time, while God alone is eternal and uncreated. We are told, however, that God can bestow an eternal nature to a creature who had a beginning in time, like us. This would include created beings such as angels as well as the souls of mankind. Eternal life can be communicated to us by God, through Jesus Christ, but it is not part of or our essential nature. It seems that the only way we can understand eternal life is to be living it, which we are told by Jesus in the Gospel of John, we can start doing in this life now. We could call this "eternity now." There is, of course, the experience of eternal life which we can have now as part of our earthly journey in time and as a foretaste of the eternal life to come.

The Gospel of John tells us that eternal life for us, is not only futuristic but also pertains to the present; that eternal life begins for us in the now moment.

In the Gospel of John 3:14–16, 36, John has Jesus telling us three times about eternal life:

> Just as Moses lifted up the snake in the wilderness, so the Son of Man must be lifted up, that everyone who believes may have eternal life in him. For God so loved the world that he gave his one and only Son, that whoever believes in him shall not perish but have eternal life. Whoever believes in the Son has eternal life, but whoever rejects the Son will not see life, (Jn. 3:14–16, 36).

> Whoever drinks the water I give them will never thirst. Indeed, the water I give them will become in them a spring of water welling up to eternal life (Jn. 4:14).

> Truly, truly I say to you, whoever hears my word and believes him who sent me has eternal life and will not be judged but has crossed over from death to life. . . . For as the Father has life in himself, so he has granted the Son also to have life in himself. . . . You study the Scriptures diligently because you think that in them you have eternal life. These are the very Scriptures that testify about me (Jn. 5:24, 26, 39).

There is so much about eternal life in several verses in Chapter 6 as Jesus tells us:

> Do not work for food that spoils, but for food that endures to eternal life, which the Son of Man will give you. . . . Then Jesus declared, "I am the bread of life. Whoever comes to me will never go hungry, and whoever believes in me will never be thirsty. . . . Everyone who sees the Son and believes in him may have eternal life, and I shall raise him on the last day. . . . Very truly I tell you, the one who believes has eternal life. I am the bread of life. Your ancestors ate the manna in the wilderness, yet they died. But here is the bread that comes down from heaven, which anyone may eat and not die. I am the living bread that came down from heaven. Whoever eats this bread will live forever. This bread is my flesh, which I will give for the life of the world. . . . It is the Spirit which gives life; the flesh counts for nothing. The words I have spoken to you—they are full of the Spirit and life" (Jn. 6:27, 35, 40, 47–53, 63).

Frankly, what Peter knew applied to himself, applies to us as well: "Lord, to whom shall we go, you have the words of eternal life (Jn. 6:68)?"

Jesus will tell us that not only do his words contain eternal life like Peter said, but He is the life. He will tell us that any and all life is in Him:

> I am the resurrection and the life. The one who believes in me will live, even though they die . . . (and) I am the way and the truth and the life. No one comes to the Father except through me (Jn. 11:25; 14:6).

Toward the end of his Gospel, John will give us his simple definition of eternal life in Chapter 17 as he tells us: "Now this is eternal life: that they know you, the only true God, and Jesus Christ, whom you have sent (Jn. 17:3)."

John will end his Gospel by telling us why he has written these many words concerning Jesus and his offer to us of eternal life here in his Gospel as he writes:

> These are written that you may believe that Jesus is the Messiah, the Son of God, and that by believing you may have life in his name (Jn. 20:31).

All of these verses we've just looked at tell us not only about having eternal life, but that it takes believing in Jesus and knowing Him as the Son of God in order to possess eternal life. Therefore, "eternal life" could also be seen as a term sometimes applied to the state and life of grace, even before our natural death. This earthly life being the initial stage of eternal life or the seed of the never-ending life of bliss which can only flower in heaven. In this sense, grace as the gift of God and of his Son can then be perceived through the power of the Holy Spirit as the very first stage of eternal life. If we believe in Jesus, love passionately, and are true to ourselves, to others, and to God, we will after death, pass into the second stage, the beautiful flower from the seed of life eternal which was sown here on earth.

As Christians, we know no other life except the one we are preparing for now and enacting in the present moment of the life in which we are living now. Eternal life is what gives this life its sacramental and infinite value. One of my favorite contemporary songs has always been "*The Rose,*" sung by Bette Midler and others, because it beautifully puts to song what I am attempting to say here concerning the seed of love and the flower of eternal life:

The Rose

> Some say, "Love. It is a river
> That drowns the tender reed."
> Some say, "Love. It is a razor
> That leaves your soul to bleed."
> Some say, "Love. It is a hunger,
> An endless aching need."
> I say, "Love. It is a flower,
> And you its only seed."
> It's the heart afraid of breaking,
> That never learns to dance.
> It's the dream afraid of waking,
> That never takes the chance.

> It's the one who won't be taken,
> Who cannot seem to give,
> And the soul afraid of dying
> That never learns to live.
> When the night has been too lonely
> And the road has been too long.
> And you think that love is only
> For the lucky and the strong.
> Just remember in the winter
> Far beneath the bitter snows
> Lies the seed that with the sun's love
> In the spring becomes the rose.[6]

As I said earlier, when we began this sub-theme on life and death: "eternity is a circle." In the circle the beginning is the end, and the end is the beginning. As we get to the end of the circle of life and enter into what for all of us will be our earthly death, we also get to the beginning of that circle at one and the same time. God is in the present now moment both in time and in the timelessness of eternity, not only as the center of the circle, but at every point in the circle. God is, was, and will be always eternal. In the Gospel of John, Jesus tells us that eternal life is in Him and for us can begin now. God has given us the promise of eternal life with Christ in this, the now moment, before the curtain comes down on our earthly life in time.[7]

NOTES

1. Ibid Ch.4 no. 3; Ibid Ch. 12 no. 4.

2. "The Lion King," John, Elton. (2004): Broadway selections, United States: (Milwaukee, WI., Walt Disney Music/Wonderland Music Co.; Distributed by Hal Leonard Corp, 2020).

3. "Eternity and Time," Hickey, Michael, Get to the End, (Lanham, MD, University Press, 2016), Ch.3, pp. 25–34.

4. Boethius, De Consol. Phil., V, VI, https://oll.libertyfund.org/titles/boethius-the-consolation-of-philosophy/simple

5. 'Augustine's Conception of Time", Herman Hausheer, The Philosophical Review, Vol. 46, No. 5 (Sep., 1937), pp. 503–512, Published by: Duke University Press on behalf of Philosophical Review, Oct. 2013, http://www.jstor.org/stable/2180833

6. Bette Midler, "The Rose" Lyrics.com. STANDS4 LLC, 2020. Web. 20 Nov. 2020. https://www.lyrics.com/lyric/31555581/Bette+Midler

7. Ibid Ch. 2 no.2.

Chapter 14

Abiding and Discipleship

ABIDING

John will use the word "abide" 34 times in his Gospel. You can surely tell it is one of his favorite words. "Abiding" is the English translation of the Greek word *meno*. It can mean to remain in the same place over a period of time, or to stay or dwell. It generally describes something or someone that remains where it is or endures. It can also imply "making yourself at home" because the root of the word *meno (mone)* means "habitat or dwelling place." More than half of the uses of *meno* in the entire Bible are used by John in his Gospel and his three letters.[1] God's love and his word abide in the hearts of all believers, whereas God's love and word do not abide in the hearts of unbelievers. For example, Jesus tells us:

> You do not have His word abiding in you, for you do not believe Him whom He sent (Jn. 5:38).[2]

In the Gospel of John, where believers or disciples are concerned, their state of "remaining" or "dwelling," or "abiding" in Christ refers to their intimate relationship with Jesus. Here is an example:

> They who eat My flesh and drink My blood abide in Me, and I in them (Jn. 6:56).

God's Word and the New Covenant in Christ's blood will abide forever because Jesus remains with us forever through the Holy Spirit abiding in all believers who follow Christ. Here the crowd first answers and then questions Jesus words:

> The crowd then answered Him, "We have heard out of the Law that the Christ is to remain forever; and how can You say, 'The Son of Man must be lifted up?' Who is this Son of Man?" (Jn. 12:34).

Those who abide in Christ remain in the light. Conversely, unbelievers who do not abide in Christ remain in darkness. Jesus, the Light of the World, tells us:

> I have come as Light into the world, so that everyone who believes in Me will not remain in darkness (Jn. 12:46).

In the Jewish temple, there were many rooms for the Israelites to worship as they entered into God's presence in the place where he dwelt. Now, Jesus has become the new temple of eternal life where God will abide with us in the Holy Spirit. In this temple Jesus is preparing a dwelling place for us and all to abide who seek the Lord. In the Last Supper discourse, here is what Jesus tells us:

> In my Father's house there are many dwelling places. If there were not, would I have told you that I am going to prepare a place for you? And if I go and prepare a place for you, I will come back again and take you to myself, so that where I am you also may be (Jn. 14:2-3).

Jesus' words have power and authority because He does not speak on His own authority, but He abides in the Father and the Father abides in Him. Here Jesus asks: "Don't you believe that I am in the Father, and that the Father is in me? The words I say to you I do not speak on my own authority. Rather, it is the Father, abiding in me, who is doing his work (Jn. 14:10)."

As for us, we abide with Jesus and the Father through the Holy Spirit whom Jesus sent from the Father to be with us and dwell within us. The idea is to remain or abide or dwell in vital union with God in Christ which is the work of the Holy Spirit abiding in us and in our lives. Here, Jesus will affirm the coming of the Paraclete to abide with all believers:

> ...The Paraclete, the Spirit of truth. The world cannot accept him, because it neither sees him nor knows him, but you know him, for he abides with you and will be in you (Jn. 14:17).

The allegory of the True Vine in John 15 is the central verse which concerns "abiding" or "remaining" in the Gospel of John. The way we abide with the Father, Jesus, and the Holy Spirit is to remain as a branch on the True Vine who is Jesus. Listen for the number of times the word "abide" or "remain" is mentioned in the allegory of the True Vine in John 15:1–10:

> I am the true vine, and my Father is the vine grower. He takes away every branch in me that does not bear fruit, and every one that does he prunes so that it bears more fruit. You are already pruned because of the word that I spoke to you.

REMAIN in me, as I REMAIN in you. Just as a branch cannot bear fruit on its own unless it REMAINS on the vine, so neither can you unless you REMAIN in me. I am the vine you are the branches. Whoever REMAINS in me and I in him will bear much fruit, because without me you can do nothing. Anyone who does not REMAIN in me will be thrown out like a branch and wither; people will gather them and throw them into the fire and they will be burned. If you REMAIN in me and my words REMAIN in you, ask for whatever you want, and it will be done for you. By this is my Father glorified, that you bear much fruit and become my disciples. As the Father loves me, so I also love you. REMAIN in my love. If you keep my commandments, you will REMAIN in my love, just as I have kept my Father's commandments and REMAIN in his love (Jn. 15:1–10).

Jesus invites us into an intimate personal relationship with Him and the Father. To allow this to happen we must abide as a branch on the True Vine. Once we abide as a branch, we can bear fruit through the Holy Spirit in relationship to Him. But we can do nothing apart from drawing our strength from the vine who is Jesus. We would only wither and die. The abiding of the Holy Spirit within us produces the spiritual fruit. Later, the Apostle Paul will tell us exactly what this spiritual fruit is in the Book of Galatians, Chapter 5. He calls them "fruit" in the singular and not "fruits" in the plural because they are all a dimension of love. The fruit of the Spirit is: "love, joy, peace, patience, kindness, generosity, faithfulness, gentleness, and self-control (Ga. 5:22)."

This fruit we bear on the vine is evidence of a life lived in Christian love. It will flourish on the branch which can only fully depend on the vine from which to draw its life. The vine and branches and the subsequent abiding are all something natural that allegorically represents something spiritual because as Thomas Aquinas has told us in his Summa: "as in the natural, so in the spiritual."[3]

The True Vine as an allegory tells us repeatedly about our abiding. It implies that we must remain as a branch united with the Father through the life of the Holy Spirit with Jesus who is the True Vine. The True Vine in John's Gospel is the best model we have for understanding both "abiding" and "discipleship" in the church because our imagination can picture the relationship between God and the disciple abiding with Jesus who is the True Vine. To paraphrase what I once heard in a homily given by a visiting Bishop from Jamaica who came to my local parish: "It all happens from root to shoot to fruit."[4]

DISCIPLESHIP

Let's talk a little bit now about the theme of discipleship which has a close relatedness to our abiding in Christ. . . . Abiding, remaining, or dwelling, can give one the impression that it involves just simple passivity, but it shouldn't. Abiding should lead to discipleship and discipleship will mean first of all, following after Jesus. The word "disciple" appears in the Gospel of John eighty times. How do we know that John likes the word? In addition to using it eighty times, he also calls himself "The Beloved Disciple."

The verb "to follow" (*akolouthó,* Gk.) is used throughout John's Gospel to denote discipleship (cf. 1:43; 8:12; 10:4–5, 15, 27; 12:26; 21:19, 22). Those who follow Jesus do not merely physically follow him but they follow his example, his manner of life and teaching. . . . Jesus in turn tells them: "Come and see (Jn. 1:39)."

We see an example of discipleship occurring right after the *Logos* Prologue in Chapter 1 of John's Gospel. This happens almost right from the beginning-from the point the Gospel opens. If we look at John 1:35–51, the scene will open with John's disciples following Jesus. Listen first for how the disciples "follow after Jesus" and then how all the disciples invite other disciples to "follow after Jesus":

> The next day John was there again with two of his disciples, and as he watched Jesus walk by, he said, "Behold, the Lamb of God." The two disciples heard what he said and followed Jesus. Jesus turned and saw them following him and said to them, "What are you looking for?" They said to him, "Rabbi" (which translated means Teacher), "where are you staying?" He said to them, "Come, and you will see." So, they went and saw where he was staying, and they stayed with him that day. It was about four in the afternoon. Andrew, the brother of Simon Peter, was one of the two who heard John and followed Jesus. He first found his own brother Simon and told him, "We have found the Messiah" (which is translated Anointed). Then he brought him to Jesus. Jesus looked at him and said, "You are Simon the son of John; you will be called Cephas" (which is translated Peter). The next day he decided to go to Galilee, and he found Philip. And Jesus said to him, "Follow me." Now Philip was from Bethsaida, the town of Andrew and Peter. Philip found Nathanael and told him, "We have found the one about whom Moses wrote in the law, and also the prophets, Jesus, son of Joseph, from Nazareth." But Nathanael said to him, "Can anything good come from Nazareth?" Philip said to him, "Come and see." Jesus saw Nathanael coming toward him and said of him, "Here is a true Israelite. There is no duplicity in him." Nathanael said to him, "How do you know me?" Jesus answered and said to him, "Before Philip called you, I saw you under the fig tree." Nathanael answered him, "Rabbi, you are the Son of God; you are the King of Israel." Jesus answered and said to him, "Do you believe because I told you that I saw

you under the fig tree? You will see greater things than this." And he said to him, "Amen, amen, I say to you, you will see the sky opened and the angels of God ascending and descending on the Son of Man" (Jn. 1: 35-51).

Do you see how abiding leads to discipleship and discipleship leads to following Jesus; then inviting others to follow Jesus? Discipleship does not just end with following Jesus. No! It should flow into believing in and bearing witness to Jesus as the Son of God or what we might call evangelizing. The Greek word for this is *"martureo"* from *mártus* which is translated as "witness." A witness is someone who has information or knowledge of something which they can bring to light or perhaps they can confirm something they have seen or heard. In its most basic sense, it refers to a legal witness who can testify, give evidence, or give testimony. They can affirm what they have seen or heard or experienced.[5]

So, being a disciple means first following Jesus but that also means bearing witness (*martureo*). What English word do you think we get from *martureo*? From this, we get our English word "martyr." The implication here is that it should involve more than learning the teachings of the Master the way a student would, but moreover, imitating the life of the Master. This is being a disciple following Jesus and bearing witness in its truest sense.

Fortunately, as modern-day disciples most of us are not called to physically be martyrs and lay down our lives for Jesus, but we are all called to do that in a spiritual sense—to sacrifice our own lives and egos, our wants and desires, to truly follow Jesus' commandment as he instructs us to: "love one another (Jn 13:34-35)."

This sacrifice is similar to what John the Baptist said and did when he decided to follow Jesus. These just might be THE best words for any disciple of Jesus to live by. When told by his disciples that Jesus was baptizing across the Jordan river from him, John then said:

He must increase, while I must decrease (Jn. 3:30).

John the Baptist sacrificed more than his ego, wants, and desires. Ultimately, he really was physically martyred for following Jesus and becoming his disciple; he lost his head in the process.

After we begin to follow Him, being a disciple of Jesus involves spiritual growth by continuing in His word as Jesus tells the Jews who believed in Him: So, Jesus was saying to those Jews who had believed Him,

If you continue in My word, then you are truly disciples of Mine; and you will know the truth, and the truth will make you free (Jn. 8:31-32).

Consequently, we should try to live out His word and His teaching by loving one another:

> A new commandment I give to you, that you love one another, even as I have loved you, that you also love one another. By this all men will know that you are My disciples, if you have love for one another (Jn. 13:34-35).

Finally, we should give evidence to those around us that we are glorifying the Father and bearing the fruit of the Spirit:

> By this is my Father glorified, that you bear much fruit and become my disciples (Jn. 15:8).

Do you remember what the fruit of the Spirit is that we discussed earlier? It is: "love, joy, peace, patience, kindness, generosity, faithfulness, gentleness, and self-control (Ga. 5:22)." It is the evidence that we truly are "abiding" in Christ and following Jesus as His "disciples."

NOTES

1. Harper, Douglas, Online Etymology Dictionary, 2001–2020, https://www.etymonline.com/search?q=abide

2. Ibid Ch.2 no. 2.

3. Summa, T. Aquinas, 1st Part of the 2nd Part, Q.68, Art. II." Knight, Kevin, New Advent Catholic Encyclopedia, 2017, https://www.newadvent.org/summa/

4. Bishop Burchell McPherson, Diocese of Montego Bay, Jamaica, Jamaica Outreach Society, (Naples, FL., St. John the Evangelist Parish. 2017).

5. "witness," Harper, Douglas, Online Etymology Dictionary, 2020, https://www.etymonline.com/search?q=witness

Chapter 15

Bread and Water

Bread is the staff of life, and all living beings need water to sustain our lives. They are both not only essential elements for the sustenance of our natural life here on earth but spiritual signs and symbols of our eternal life in Jesus Christ. Jesus, as the Sacrament of God, is the "living bread" and the "water of life."

BREAD

The theme of "bread" takes up all of Chapter 6 of John's Gospel. It begins as the fourth of the seven signs in the Book of Signs. This is referred to as the "Multiplication of the Loaves" which then flows into the Bread of Life Discourse which begins in Ch. 6:22. Let's look now at The Bread of Life Discourse:

> The next day, the crowd that remained across the sea saw that there had been only one boat there, and that Jesus had not gone along with his disciples in the boat, but only his disciples had left. Other boats came from Tiberias near the place where they had eaten the bread when the Lord gave thanks. When the crowd saw that neither Jesus nor his disciples were there, they themselves got into boats and came to Capernaum looking for Jesus. And when they found him across the sea, they said to him, "Rabbi, when did you get here?" Jesus answered them and said, "Amen, amen, I say to you, you are looking for me not because you saw signs but because you ate the loaves and were filled. Do not work for food that perishes but for the food that endures for eternal life, which the Son of Man will give you. For on him the Father, God, has set his seal." So, they said to him, "What can we do to accomplish the works of God?" Jesus answered and said to them, "This is the work of God, that you believe in the one he sent." So, they said to him, "What sign can you do, that we may see and believe in you? What can you do? Our ancestors ate manna in the desert, as it is written 'He gave them bread from heaven to eat.'" So, Jesus said to them, "Amen, amen, I

say to you, it was not Moses who gave the bread from heaven; my Father gives you the true bread from heaven. For the bread of God is that which comes down from heaven and gives life to the world." So, they said to him, "Sir, give us this bread always." Jesus said to them, "I am the bread of life; whoever comes to me will never hunger, and whoever believes in me will never thirst. But I told you that although you have seen [me], you do not believe. Everything that the Father gives me will come to me, and I will not reject anyone who comes to me, because I came down from heaven not to do my own will but the will of the one who sent me. And this is the will of the one who sent me, that I should not lose anything of what he gave me, but that I should raise it [on] the last day. For this is the will of my Father, that everyone who sees the Son and believes in him may have eternal life, and I shall raise him [on] the last day." The Jews murmured about him because he said, "I am the bread that came down from heaven," and they said, "Is this not Jesus, the son of Joseph? Do we not know his father and mother? Then how can he say, 'I have come down from heaven'?" Jesus answered and said to them, "Stop murmuring among yourselves. No one can come to me unless the Father who sent me draw him, and I will raise him on the last day. It is written in the prophets: 'They shall all be taught by God.' Everyone who listens to my Father and learns from him comes to me. Not that anyone has seen the Father except the one who is from God; he has seen the Father. Amen, amen, I say to you, whoever believes has eternal life. I am the bread of life. Your ancestors ate the manna in the desert, but they died; this is the bread that comes down from heaven so that one may eat it and not die. I am the living bread that came down from heaven; whoever eats this bread will live forever; and the bread that I will give is my flesh for the life of the world." The Jews quarreled among themselves, saying, "How can this man give us [his] flesh to eat?" Jesus said to them, "Amen, amen, I say to you, unless you eat the flesh of the Son of Man and drink his blood, you do not have life within you. Whoever eats my flesh and drinks my blood has eternal life, and I will raise him on the last day. For my flesh is true food, and my blood is true drink. Whoever eats my flesh and drinks my blood remains in me and I in him. Just as the living Father sent me and I have life because of the Father, so also the one who feeds on me will have life because of me. This is the bread that came down from heaven. Unlike your ancestors who ate and still died, whoever eats this bread will live forever" (Jn. 6:22-58).[1]

The word "bread" in John is from the Greek word, *artos,* from which we get our English word "artisan." Have you heard of artisan bread before? It is bread crafted using quality ingredients.[2] Following the use of bread as a bodily food in the feeding of the multitudes as one of the seven signs, Jesus will tell the multitudes that they should not be following him because they have had their fill of the bread. Furthermore, they shouldn't be working for the bread that perishes but for that which leads to eternal life. They were looking for more temporal and worldly satisfaction of filling their stomachs with more bread. He will then begin to talk more about spiritual food while comparing himself to the "Bread of Life—the Living Bread" which came down from heaven.

It was believed by the Hebrews that when the Messiah came, he would reproduce the ancient Moses miracle of the distribution of manna which came down from heaven to feed the Israelites in the desert. Jesus will tell them that it was not Moses who gave them this bread, it was His Father. Following that statement by Jesus, the Bread of Life Discourse would begin, and Jesus would reveal himself to them as being the "Living Bread" which came down from Heaven. Unlike the earthly bread which is corruptible because it does not have life within itself, the heavenly bread which came down from heaven is incorruptible. Material bread would only sustain life for a time because it would eventually lead to death, but the living bread would do much more than that. It would not just sustain life it would give life, because Jesus' flesh is united to the word of God, making it the "bread of life" and consequently life-giving. As had been said in the Old Testament Book of Deuteronomy: "Man does not live by bread alone, but by every word which comes from the mouth of God (Dt. 8:3)."

Now with all that flesh and blood to eat, no wonder some of the disciples exclaimed at the end of the discourse: "This is a hard saying, who can listen to it (Jn. 6:60)?"

Peter, recognizing the situation made the smart odds-on choice when he said to Jesus: "Lord, to whom shall we go? You have the words of eternal life (Jn. 6:69)."

Bread is both a sign and a symbol, but it is more particularly closer to a symbol in John. By definition, a symbol is a sign which embodies what it signifies.[3] When Jesus says: "I Am the Bread of Life" and "I Am the Living Bread," He is embodying the sign of bread. As a sign, the bread is something that sustains life. As the symbol, Jesus, as the living bread, is the very sustenance and giver of life itself—eternal life. To take that even one step further, the meaning of the word symbol is close but not as descriptive and relevant to our discussion on the theme of bread as the word "sacrament." What do you think a sacrament is? Please bear in mind that we are not necessarily talking about the formal Sacraments of the Catholic Church, i.e., Baptism, Eucharist, Holy Orders etc. So, what generally is a sacrament? By definition, a sacrament is a visible grace-bearing sign or symbol of an invisible reality. The reality always relates to God's presence because all reality is potentially the bearer of God's presence.[4] What John is trying to show us here is that beyond the sign and symbol of bread is the Sacrament who is Jesus Himself as both the Living Bread or Bread of Life and the Sacrament of God's presence among His people. Jesus is both the symbol of the Living Bread and the Sacrament of the Living God.

Finally, in John Ch. 6:53–58, it is hard not to see the allusion that John is making to the bread of the Eucharist in the early church. Once again, if we go back to where we began the theme of bread and reread The Bread of Life Discourse-we see at the end of that section the following:

> Jesus said to them, "Amen, amen, I say to you, unless you eat the flesh of the Son of Man and drink his blood, you do not have life within you. Whoever eats my flesh and drinks my blood has eternal life, and I will raise him on the last day. For my flesh is true food, and my blood is true drink. Whoever eats my flesh and drinks my blood remains in me and I in him. Just as the living Father sent me and I have life because of the Father, so also the one who feeds on me will have life because of me. This is the bread that came down from heaven. Unlike your ancestors who ate and still died, whoever eats this bread will live forever" (Jn. 6:53-58).

When Jesus says: "You must eat the flesh of the Son of Man and drink his blood," as we learned a little earlier in John, the Son of Man title originated in the Old Testament Book of Daniel. It described someone who was essentially a messenger from heaven and one in whom both God and mankind meet. It is fitting that Jesus would identify the Eucharistic Bread with himself as the Son of Man and with his own flesh and blood. John is one of the first to establish that the reality of the Christ life is received in the Eucharistic Bread, the reception of which establishes communion of life between Christ and the Christian. This is the reason why Catholics believe that it is God's real presence in the Eucharist.[5]

As was discussed previously, it was believed by Israel that when the Messiah came, He would reproduce the miracle of the manna with which God fed the Israelites in the desert. On a literal level, the truth is that the fathers in the desert ate manna and died. The bread Jesus gives them comes from heaven and they will not die. The bread of which Jesus speaks is the true bread of God of which the manna the Israelites received in the desert was only a faint type. The Living Bread is pre-eminently a Eucharistic Sacrament of Life. As we saw in John 6:54, here the type of life Jesus is talking about is eternal when he says: "Whoever eats my flesh and drinks my blood has eternal life, and I will raise him on the last day (Jn. 6:54)."

The only question that remains for us once we hear this is: Do we believe this? If we do, then as the song goes that is sung at Catholic mass, we must: "Look beyond the bread you eat; see your Savior and your Lord."[6]

WATER

Let's move on to the theme of water which, like bread, is another sustainer of life. The theme of Bread and the theme of Water in the Gospel of John have many similarities. One simple one is that you don't make bread without water. Without water, you would just have flour. Like bread, water is necessary to sustain natural life, and just like bread which will leave you hungry again, water will leave you thirsty again. Another striking similarity is that exactly before the Bread of Life Discourse which we discussed in Chapter 6, the disciples saw Jesus walking on the water.

This was the fifth of seven signs, if you recall, in John's Book of Signs. Let's look at this particular sign again:

> When it was evening, his disciples went down to the sea, embarked in a boat and went across the sea to Capernaum. It had already grown dark, and Jesus had not yet come to them. The sea was stirred up because a strong wind was blowing. When they had rowed about three or four miles, they saw Jesus walking on the sea and coming near the boat, and they began to be afraid. But he said to them, "It is I. Do not be afraid." They wanted to take him into the boat, but the boat immediately arrived at the shore to which they were heading (Jn. 6: 16-21).

What immediately follows this miraculous water scene is The Bread of Life Discourse. What is significant about that? Well, it shows that Jesus has the power of almighty God. God alone can control nature, including the ruling of the seas. Just as God controlled the parting of the Red Sea for the Israelites, John will have Jesus controlling the sea and walking on it which only God can do. Only God has that power. Additionally, only God can be the living water like only He can be the bread of life.

To go back to the beginning of this Gospel, right after the *Logos* Prologue in John Chapter 1—the scene opens in this Gospel with John the Baptist baptizing in water beyond the Jordan river. This is followed in Chapter 2 by Jesus' very first miracle in the Book of Signs. What was the first miracle-do you remember? It was the wedding at Cana where Jesus turns the water into wine. Then shortly after in Chapter 3, Jesus will tell Nicodemus: "Truly, truly, I say to you, unless one is born of water and the Spirit, he cannot enter the Kingdom of God (Jn. 3:5)."

Sequentially, the theme of water will flow (pun intended) into Chapter 4 which concerns the woman at the well and more water as a theme. This time "Living Water—" the water which bubbles up to eternal life. Let's look at this:

> A woman of Samaria came to draw water. Jesus said to her, "Give me a drink."
> His disciples had gone into the town to buy food. The Samaritan woman said

to him, "How can you, a Jew, ask me, a Samaritan woman, for a drink?" (For Jews use nothing in common with Samaritans.) Jesus answered and said to her, "If you knew the gift of God and who is saying to you, 'Give me a drink,' you would have asked him, and he would have given you living water." [The woman] said to him, "Sir, you do not even have a bucket and the well is deep; where then can you get this living water? Are you greater than our father Jacob, who gave us this well and drank from it himself with his children and his flocks?" Jesus answered and said to her, "Everyone who drinks this water will be thirsty again; but whoever drinks the water I shall give will never thirst; the water I shall give will become in him a spring of water welling up to eternal life." The woman said to him, "Sir, give me this water, so that I may not be thirsty or have to keep coming here to draw water" (Jn. 4:7-15).

In so many ways the woman at the well in Chapter 4 is very similar to the Bread of Life Discourse in Chapter 6. The water doesn't stop flowing through the chapters of John. In Chapter 5, the poor paralytic man is waiting by the pool of Bethsaida for someone to put him in to be healed once the angel stirs up the water in the sheep's pool. The healing of the paralytic was the third of the seven signs in John's Book of Signs; it also involves the sub-theme of Water. We saw then in Chapter 6 how Jesus walked on water showing His power over nature. So now we are through the first 6 chapters and as we move into Chapter 7, Jesus will offer living water once again as he did to the woman at the well. This time, Jesus is at the Feast of Tabernacles. Listen to what he declares concerning not just water but "rivers of living water":

On the last and greatest day of the feast, Jesus stood up and exclaimed, "Let anyone who thirsts come to me and drink. Whoever believes in me, as scripture says: 'Rivers of living water will flow from within him.' He said this in reference to the Spirit that those who came to believe in him were to receive. There was, of course, no Spirit yet, because Jesus had not yet been glorified" (Jn. 7:37-39).

Verse 39 is a giveaway by John. He tells us that the "Living Water" is really the Holy Spirit which Jesus will send from the Father following his glorification. In Chapter 8 there is no immediate continuation of the water theme; we have to move over to Chapter 9. Here we have another miracle which continues the water theme as Jesus spits on the ground, heals the blind man, and then tells him:

"While I am in the world, I am the light of the world." When he had said this, he spat on the ground and made clay with the saliva, and smeared the clay on his eyes, and said to him, "Go wash in the Pool of Siloam" (which means Sent). So, he went and washed, and came back able to see. (Jn. 9:5-7).

Do you see how water is involved in many of the signs, in many of what Jesus calls his "works"? Even if we don't include Jesus' spittle as water, water is still used here to have the blind man, who has been blind since birth wash in the Pool of Siloam.

The water rushes by Chapters 10, 11, & 12 until we get to Chapter 13 where Jesus will wash the feet of the disciples. Let's look at that particular scene:

> Then he poured water into a basin and began to wash the disciples' feet and dry them with the towel around his waist. He came to Simon Peter, who said to him, "Master, are you going to wash my feet?" Jesus answered and said to him, "What I am doing, you do not understand now, but you will understand later." Peter said to him, "You will never wash my feet." Jesus answered him, "Unless I wash you, you will have no inheritance with me." Simon Peter said to him, "Master, then not only my feet, but my hands and head as well." Jesus said to him, "Whoever has bathed has no need except to have his feet washed, for he is clean all over; so you are clean, but not all" (Jn. 13:5-10).

Jesus washing the disciples' feet is a model which would prefigure the humiliating death Jesus would suffer in crucifixion. It will symbolize the washing away of our sins. Israel had been waiting for a Messiah-King in the line of David; however, the Messiah they had expected would come in power and great glory. They did not recognize Jesus as the Messiah because he had turned the whole power and glory idea on its head—A servant King washing his disciple's feet? A crucified Messiah? Ridiculous! To the Jews this was pure folly.

In Chapter 19, it is just after Jesus tells everyone from the wood of the cross: "I thirst (Jn. 19:28)." He is not given water but common wine. Jesus then bows his head and says: "It is finished (Jn. 19:30)." Jesus shows his power by giving up his Spirit, thus opening the door to eternal life for us. He would give us a glimpse of His true power and glory following the crucifixion and before the resurrection. Immediately following Jesus' crucifixion, as Jesus lay dead on the wood of the cross, we get our last look at the theme of water in John's Gospel: "But when they came to Jesus and saw that he was already dead, they did not break his legs, but one soldier thrust his lance into his side, and immediately blood and water flowed out (Jn. 19:34)." In the blood and water flowing from Jesus' side, there may be some symbolic sacramental references to the developing understanding in the early Christian church of the later Sacraments of Eucharist and Baptism.

Water is essential for all life on earth. Human beings are made up of 60 percent water in a human body, and as for blood, around 55 percent of blood is made up of plasma. Plasma is 90 percent water, so water (and blood) is certainly essential for sustaining our human life. Jesus' human life on earth had just ended and this was the medical evidence of it, but John is seeing much more significance in the water and blood event.[7] Thomas Aquinas in his later commentary on John's Gospel tells us the significance of this water and blood flowing from Jesus' side. Aquinas' thoughts are very profound, and his words are so much more eloquent than mine, so let's listen to what Aquinas says about this event in his commentary on John's Gospel:

> At once there came out blood and water. This is a remarkable miracle, that blood should flow from the body of a dead person where blood congeals. And if someone says that this was because the body was still warm, the flow of the water cannot be explained without a miracle, since this was pure water. This outpouring of blood and water happened so that Christ might show that he was truly human. For human beings have a twofold composition: one from the elements and the other from the humors (bodily fluids). One of these elements is water, and blood is the main humor (bodily fluid). We are cleansed from our sins by his blood, which is the price of our redemption…And we are cleansed from our stains by the water, which is the bath of our rebirth. . . . And so, it is these two things which are especially associated with two sacraments: water with the sacrament of Baptism, and blood with the Eucharist. Or, both blood and water are associated with the Eucharist because in this sacrament water is mixed with wine, although water is not of the substance of the sacrament.[8]

What Aquinas relates is confirmed for us today in modern times by the *Jerome Biblical Commentary* which is one of the most trusted tools used in Biblical scholarship. Here is what the *JBC* has to say about the blood and water event in John's Gospel:

> The phenomenon of Jesus human death can be expressed medically, but John is more interested in the event of the blood and water as a sign. With Christ's death and the handing over of the Spirit, already signified in vs 30, the life-giving work of the church begins and hence the church can be said, in a sense, to have been born from the wounded side of Christ. Water and blood are signs of salvation and it is most likely that John expected his readers to think specifically of the Sacraments of Baptism and the Eucharist.[9]

In many ways the Middle Ages *commentary of Thomas Aquinas* and the Modern-Day *Jerome Biblical Commentary* concur on the significance of the blood and water in John's Gospel as a medical phenomenon which confirmed Jesus' human death as the handing over of the Spirit occurred. Furthermore, they also appear to concur on the sacramental significance of the blood and water as being symbolic of the later development of the church's Sacramental rites of Baptism and the Eucharist. These were practiced, but not formally in place at the time that John wrote his Gospel. They were initiated more formally in the second century as part of the Apostolic Tradition which was handed down and fully formalized at the Council of Trent in 1545 AD.[10] The Christian Church, both at the time John wrote his Gospel as well as today, was to be the Sacrament of the Kingdom of God on earth, the promise-keeper of eternal life, and the salvific guardian of Jesus' life-giving Spirit. While in the meantime, the "River of Living Water" continues to flow downstream, ultimately purifying the ocean of life.

NOTES

1. Ibid Ch. 2 no. 2.
2. Douglas Harper, Etymology Online Dictionary, 2001, https://www.etymonline.com/search?q=artisan.
3. "Symbol", Ibid Ch.3 no. 7, also McBrien, Richard, Catholicism, (San Fran., CA, Harper Collins., 1966), p. 1252.
4. "Sacrament", Ibid Ch. 3 no. 7, also Ibid Ch.3 no. 7, also McBrien, Richard, Catholicism, (San Fran., CA, Harper Collins, San Fran., 1966, pp. 9–11; 264–266; 790–800; 1108–1113; 1196–1199.
5. McBrien, Richard, Catholicism, (San Fran, CA, Harper Collins., 1966), pp. 590–591; 796–830; 1068–1069.
6. Daryl Ducotte, Composer, Gary Daigle, Arrangement, 1969, https://www.godsongs.net/2017/06/look-beyond-the-bread-you-eat-see-your-saviour.html
7. Ibid Ch. 4 no. 3, "Water and Blood," Brown, Raymond, JBC, (Englewood Cliffs, NJ, Prentice-Hall Publishing, 1969), Sec. 172, p. 462C. "Blood," Lockard Conlcy and Robert S. Schwartz, Blood, Encyclopedia Britannica, https://www.britannica.com/science/blood-biochemistry, accessed November 21, 2020.
8. Ibid Ch.4 no. 4, Aquinas, Thomas, Summa, 3rd part Q. 66.
9. Ibid Ch. 4 no.3, Ibid Ch. 15 no. 7, pp. 462; Sec. 63:172).
10. "The Apostolic Fathers." Peterson, John Bertram, The Catholic Encyclopedia. Vol. 1. (NY, New York: Robert Appleton Company, 1907). 21 Nov. 2020 http://www.newadvent.org/cathen/01637a.htm. Also, Council of Trent, https://www.newadvent.org/cathen/15030c.htm

Chapter 16

Love

The Jerome Biblical Commentary on the Bible tells us that no new Testament author has had a greater emphasis on the virtue of love than John the Evangelist who reveals Jesus as the incarnation of the Father's divine love for us.[1] The word "love" appears 57 times in the Gospel of John, more often than in the other three Gospels combined.

We learned earlier in Chapter 6 of this book as we studied the Major Theme of the Epilogue (John Chapter 21) that there are a few different words in the Greek language which translate the word "love." There is *"eros,"* which is a lustful kind of love, and *philios* which implies affection, brotherly love, or companionship. However, the word, *agape,* in the Greek which is translated as "love" is mentioned thirty times in the Gospel of John. When John uses the Greek word *agape,* it is intended to mean loving the way God loves, unconditionally and sacrificially. It is the highest, purest, and noblest form of love. Most often, John will use the verb form of the word *(agapeo)* to imply loving in action initiated by freedom of choice rather than love as a relational noun and an emotion or affection. Love is best communicated by loving actions not loving words. This differs from *(phileo* Gk.) which implies affection or a brotherly love and also from the Greek word *eros* which is never used by John. *Agape* is the very essence and existence of God. Loving is within the nature of God Himself and is best expressed by God loving us so much that He gave his only begotten and beloved Son Jesus as an act of loving in action. Christian love is dynamically active and is modeled after God's love. It began when Jesus, God's beloved Son, showed his act of loving the Father and us by laying down his life at the cross. We then show our loving in action by obediently interiorizing God's highest commandment and loving God and one another.[2]

There are many Americans who watch sporting events such as football, baseball, soccer, basketball, and golf. There are so many sports to watch either live in the stands at the event, or at home in front of the television. I'm sure you have noticed that some Christians attempt to present a gospel witness in stadiums, arenas, on golf courses, etc. and perhaps you have seen the signs held up in the crowd. Most commonly, the signs have this short message: "Jn. 3:16."

The idea is that people will know or find out that "Jn." is shorthand for the Gospel of John and that "3:16" means Chapter 3 verse 16 of John's Gospel. The hope of the evangelizing sign holder is that the Holy Spirit will touch the person seeing the sign and move them interiorly to merely pick up a Bible and read this one verse in the Gospel of John. The verse reads:

> For God so loved the world, that he gave his only Son, that whoever believes in him should not perish but have eternal life (Jn. 3:16).[3]

It is certainly possible and has happened occasionally, that someone who simply reads that one verse is touched by the Holy Spirit present in the word of God and in the believer and that person is then drawn into a more loving relationship with the Lord. That is the reason why Christian evangelizers do this. Of course, it is not as personal as someone sharing the Gospel face to face, but this method does occasionally work because large numbers of people see the verse and wonder about it.

John points to Jesus' death on the cross and his glorification as an example of the type of love that Jesus expects of us as his disciples (cf. Jn. 3:16; 15:12–13). John tries to make it clear to us that to understand Jesus' concept of love requires understanding more than what Jesus taught in his Gospel. It requires understanding Jesus' loving actions and its implications even in those Gospel episodes that John describes that don't use any literal terminology which defines love. Some examples are Jesus as the Good Shepard laying down his life for the sheep (Jn. 10:1–21), the washing of the disciple's feet (Jn. 13:1–31), and ultimately Jesus' crucifixion and death (Jn. Chapters 18–20)—these are all perfect examples of love. They are not merely loving words but loving in action.

Because of this, it is not at all possible to separate the sub-theme of Love from any of the other four Major themes, or any other sub-theme we find in the Gospel of John. Loving is intertwined with every other theme we would uncover that John highlights in his Gospel. This is especially true of any theme which discusses relationship within the persons of the Trinity, as well as any relationship we have with the Godhead as Christian believers. Furthermore, it is also true of any relationship we have with one another as disciples of Christ. You can't take love out of any theme in John's Gospel and still call it the Gospel of Jesus Christ according to John. John will tell us later in one of his epistles that the reason for this is because: "God is Love (1 Jn. 4:8)."

Let's look at some of the verses on love in John's Gospel. For example:

> For the Father loves the Son and shows him all that he is doing. Yes, and he will show him even greater works than these, so that you may marvel (Jn. 5:20).

> Jesus said to them, "If God were your Father, you would love me, for I have come here from God. I have not come on my own; God sent me" (Jn. 8:42).

Later, Jesus will tell Thomas, the doubting disciple: "see me; see the Father." So, then it follows, love me; love the Father. John will also show us here that God did not just love the world in general, God loved some specific people too: "So, the sisters sent word to Jesus, 'Lord, the one you love is sick.'—Now Jesus loved Martha and her sister and Lazarus (Jn. 11:3, 5)."

Jesus loved Lazarus and his sisters Martha and Mary so much he wept right along with them, causing the Jews to say: "See how he loved him (Jn 11:36)!"

In Ch. 12, Jesus will tell us that if we love our life in this world, we do it at the expense of our eternal life and ultimately, we will lose it. Furthermore, that if we love human praise and prefer it to praise from God, we do it at the expense of drawing closer to God's love. Jesus tells us: "Anyone who loves their life will lose it, while anyone who hates their life in this world will keep it for eternal life (Jn 12:25)." And: "…for they loved human praise more than praise from God (Jn. 12:43)."

There is a kind of a turnabout here in these two verses because Jesus is saying to us that some loving, especially of our worldly life and of our own egos, could cause us to lose out on eternal life. Jesus loves us with an eternal love and showed us so with loving actions, right up to the cross and the end of his earthly human life. At the very beginning of Ch. 13 John will tell us:

> It was just before the Passover Festival. Jesus knew that the hour had come for him to leave this world and go to the Father. Having loved his own who were in the world, he loved them to the end (Jn. 13:1).

You have heard it said many times in many ways: "love is eternal—love never ends—and in the end, love is all there is (1 Cor. 13)."

As was the case with Martha, Mary, and Lazarus, Jesus showed his love by especially loving particular people in this world--one of whom was also John the Beloved, the writer of this Gospel:

> One of them, the disciple whom Jesus loved, was reclining next to him (Jn. 13:23).

LOVE AND OBEDIENCE

Jesus will first tell us that it is because the Father loves the Son and has given everything over to Him, we should believe in Jesus as God's Son, and in doing so, the Father has promised us eternal life. If we do not obey Jesus' commands, we will not see life and will ultimately experience the wrath of God. Here, Jesus will both encourage and caution us:

> The Father loves the Son and has given everything over to him. Whoever believes in the Son has eternal life, but whoever disobeys the Son will not see life, but the wrath of God remains upon him (Jn. 3:35-36).

Because Jesus is the Good Shepard, he will choose to lay down His life for the sheep, but this is to take it up again. It is in His power to lay it down and take it up. However, He is acting in loving obedience to the command that the Father has given Him, and for doing this we are told that the Father loves Him:

> This is why the Father loves me, because I lay down my life in order to take it up again. No one takes it from me, but I lay it down on my own. I have power to lay it down, and power to take it up again. This command I have received from my Father (Jn. 10:17-18).

Jesus will also advise us that He is obedient to the Father's will as it is the Father who loves Him who is commanding Him what to say and how to speak because the Father's commandment is eternal life:

> I did not speak on my own, but the Father who sent me commanded me what to say and speak. And I know that his commandment is eternal life. So, what I say, I say as the Father told me (Jn. 12:49-50).

Jesus shows us that the path to peace is loving obedience to the Father's will rather than our own self-will and self-interest. In this way we can dwell in peace first with those around us in our own immediate circle and only then can we eventually be at peace with the world.

Jesus gave us a new commandment that would allow us to be obedient to the Father's will as He was and that is to "love one another" as He loved us. Adherence to Jesus' new commandment will not only open the way as a path to peace but to the gift of eternal life which the Father offers us. Loving one another will show the world that we are disciples of Jesus Christ. Jesus commands us:

A new command I give you: Love one another. As I have loved you, so you must love one another. By this everyone will know that you are my disciples, if you love one another (Jn. 13:34-35).

Unlike the synoptic Gospels, in John's Gospel Jesus doesn't talk much about loving your neighbor like loving God and not even loving your enemies as those three Gospels imply. John has given us the new commandment Jesus left us, which was very simply: "love one another."

But it's not as simple as that, the commandment was to love one another, but it goes on to say "as I have loved you." Consequently, we show our love for Jesus by keeping His commandment to love one another as He loved us. It will be the Holy Spirit who will be our Advocate, sent by Jesus from the Father, who will be helping us to keep His commandment of love:

"If you love me, you will keep my commandments. And I will ask the Father, and he will give you another Advocate to be with you always the Spirit of truth, which the world cannot accept, because it neither sees nor knows it. But you know it, because it remains with you, and will be in you. . . . Whoever has my commandments and observes them is the one who loves me. And whoever loves me will be loved by my Father, and I will love him and reveal myself to him." . . . "Whoever loves me will keep my word, and my Father will love him, and we will come to him and make our dwelling with him...Whoever does not love me does not keep my words; yet the word you hear is not mine but that of the Father who sent me. "I have told you this while I am with you. . . . If you loved me, you would rejoice that I am going to the Father; for the Father is greater than I . . . the world must know that I love the Father and that I do just as the Father has commanded me. Get up, let us go" (Jn.14: 15-17, 21, 23-24, 29, 31).

As the Father loves Jesus, so Jesus loves us. We show our demonstrated love for Jesus and the Father by being obedient to Jesus' commands as Jesus was obedient to the Father. If we do this, we will not only be loved by Jesus and the Father, but they will remain with us and dwell with us in the Holy Spirit. Jesus will then repeat a second and third time that His commandment is for us to love one another as He loves us. If we obey Jesus' commandment to love one another as He loved us, we will then be referred to not only as Jesus' disciples, but as Jesus' friends. Because we are chosen as Jesus' friends, we have been appointed to go and bear the fruit of the Holy Spirit:

If you keep my commandments, you will remain in my love, just as I have kept my Father's commandments and remain in his love. "I have told you this so that my joy may be in you and your joy may be complete. This is my commandment: love one another as I love you. No one has greater love than this, to lay down one's life for one's friends. You are my friends if you do what I command you. I no longer call you slaves, because a slave does not know what his master is doing. I have called you friends, because I have told you everything I have heard from my Father. It was not you who chose me, but I who chose you and appointed you to go and bear fruit that will remain, so that whatever you ask the Father in my name he may give you. This I command you: love one another (Jn. 15:10-17).

Jesus' obedient love for the Father and for us as His friends leads Him to His glorification at the crucifixion which tells us more about His love than any words. Furthermore, as He had promised us, he lay down His life only to take it up again.

Like Mary Magdalene following Jesus' resurrection, we are told to not hold on to Jesus but be happy he is going to the Father. Jesus' departure will allow the Holy Spirit to be sent to us from the Father so that the entire Godhead, Father, Son, and Holy Spirit can then make their home in us as believers. Only then can we rise up! with Jesus. When Jesus departs, the Paraclete is sent from the Father through the Son. It is then that the Trinity makes their home within us, including us in their circle of love. Father, Son, and Holy Spirit, a complete and unifying relationship which then includes us as adopted children of God. When we say the words, "Come Holy Spirit," we are inviting not just the Holy Spirit, but the Father and the Son as well to come and live in a relationship of love with us. The Trinity will not come separately to love in us. Jesus will tell us about this Trinitarian love dwelling within us in this way:

> I in them and you in me—so that they may be brought to complete unity. Then the world will know that you sent me and have loved them even as you have loved me. Father, I want those you have given me to be with me where I am, and to see my glory, the glory you have given me because you loved me before the creation of the world...I have made you known to them and will continue to make you known in order that the love you have for me may be in them and that I myself may be in them (Jn. 17:23-24, 26).

At the foot of the cross, the love that Jesus has for his mother makes her not only His beloved disciple's mother, but as Jesus' adopted brothers and sisters in Christ, our mother as well. John writes:

> When Jesus saw his mother and the disciple there whom he loved, he said to his mother, "Woman, behold, your son." Then he said to the disciple, "Behold, your mother." And from that hour the disciple took her into his home (Jn. 19:26-27).

As one of His final acts, Jesus' handing over the Beloved Disciple to His mother and she to him, creates a new relationship based on love. John is seen as a metaphor and an icon for all believers throughout time who will be united in love to Jesus and His mother. Mary is, of course, a model of not only the first church, but also an icon of the new church founded on the spirit of love. The spiritual motherhood of Mary began with her "yes" to the Holy Spirit and the subsequent birth of Jesus. It continues at the foot of the cross of Christ as Jesus gives her to John as his mother and Mary to John. That act of love will soon extend to us, as Mary, our new mother and John our new brother gather with all the Apostles in the upper room on Pentecost. The Holy Spirit, which Jesus promised to send from the Father, is then poured out on all believers as the new Christian church continues to broaden Jesus' circle of love extending to all time.

Chapter 21, the Epilogue, if you will recall, was probably not part of the original Gospel of John, but a later addition. It was written at a subsequent time either by John himself, or as it is believed more likely by a disciple of John. It contains these few verses which is a dialogue between the Lord Jesus and the apostle Peter and is a very telling love story:

> When they had finished eating, Jesus said to Simon Peter, "Simon son of John, do you love me more than these?" "Yes, Lord," he said, "you know that I love you." Jesus said, "Feed my lambs." Again, Jesus said, "Simon son of John, do you love me?" He answered, "Yes, Lord, you know that I love you." Jesus said, "Take care of my sheep." The third time he said to him, "Simon son of John, do you love me?" Peter was hurt because Jesus asked him the third time, "Do you love me?" He said, "Lord, you know all things; you know that I love you." Jesus said, "Feed my sheep" (Jn. 21:15-17).

First, the triple love question is reminiscent of Peter's triple denial of Jesus as the cock crowed. What has always intrigued me about this passage is that our English word, "love" does not give us a complete and full understanding of the actual conversation between Jesus and Peter. Recall at the beginning of our discussion on the theme of Love, I said that there were a few Greek words in the Bible which translate the word "love." There is *eros*, a kind of lustful love, *philios* meaning affection, brotherly love, or companionship, and *agape*, which is God's unconditional and sacrificial love. Now, listen to the translation of those verses once again while substituting the different Greek words for our English word, "love.":

> When they had finished breakfast, Jesus said to Simon Peter, "Simon, son of John, do you *agape* me more than these?" Peter said to him, "Yes, Lord; you know that I *phileo* you." He said to him, "Feed my lambs." He said to him a second time, "Simon, son of John, do you *agape* me?" Peter said to him, "Yes, Lord; you know that I *phileo* you." He said to him, "Tend my sheep." He said to him the third time, "Simon, son of John, do you *phileo* me?" Peter was grieved because he said to him the third time, "Do you *phileo* me?" and Peter said to

him, "Lord, you know everything; you know that I *phileo* you." Jesus said to him, "Feed my sheep." (Jn. 21:15-17).

You get a very different vibe and much more of a true understanding about the conversation between the Lord Jesus and Peter that way, don't you? Jesus wants Peter to have *agape,* God's unconditional love for him. However, Jesus is not able to get that as an answer perhaps because of Peter sensing that it may mean his martyrdom. Therefore, Peter is unwilling to commit to the self-sacrificing and unconditional love that Jesus possesses and is asking of him in return.

Ultimately, Jesus will accept Peter's level of loving him for the time being. Jesus is willing even to accept Peter's *"phileos"* love for now. God always meets us where we are, but always calls us to greater love.[4] Jesus will then tell Peter about his own martyrdom and how he will glorify God. Jesus will simply say to him: "Follow me (Jn. 21:19)."

Shortly after being told about his own future martyrdom, Peter will ask Jesus about the Beloved Disciple, John, following behind and what will happen to him. The dialogue takes on much greater significance if John, the beloved disciple, had already died. John's death would have signaled an end to the Apostolic generation completely before the Parousia (second coming). The disciple of John who may have been redacting and writing these additional verses at a later date would have been looking at John's death in the rear-view mirror and addressing a crisis of faith in the Christian community at that time.

"Do you love me?" as a question of Peter is a question Jesus puts to us as well. The dialogue in these few verses indicates that Jesus wants us to pay no attention to who is following Him and what happens to them in the end. If we truly love Jesus, we should only be focused on our own loving walk with Him regardless of what happens with others or what others may do or not do until he comes again in glory (Jn. 21:21–23).

LOVE AND FEAR

John does discuss the subject of fear a little in his Gospel and although it probably should not qualify as a separate theme, I believe that it should be mentioned here along with the theme of love. The reasons for this are threefold:

1. The phrase "do not be afraid" or "fear not" is the most oft repeated statement in the entire Bible. It occurs some three hundred times in the Old and New Testament. We can draw at least a few conclusions from this.

2. In the Judeo-Christian world, there were times when the people of God were afraid and needed some loving comfort or were urged to confront their fears.
3. Because the words "do not be afraid" come most often from the mouth of God in scripture, it would seem that the Lord doesn't want us to be afraid or let the manifestation of fear be a greater motivator than our love for Him and one another.

John gives evidence through his writings, particularly in his letters, that he believes that fear is an opposite of love. Although not emphasized a great deal in his Gospel, John places considerable emphasis on "love and fear" in his first Epistle (1 John).

FEAR IN THE GOSPEL OF JOHN

Many who were drawn to Christ in John's Gospel were often worried that the religious classes and synagogue officials were going to punish them for their beliefs, sometimes to the extent of expelling them from the synagogue or having them arrested, So in the Gospel of John, "fear of the Jews" is something John will speak to on four separate occasions:

1. The Crowd

"The Jews were looking for him at the feast and saying, 'Where is he?' And there was considerable murmuring about him in the crowds. Some said, 'He is a good man,' while others said, 'No; on the contrary, he misleads the crowd.' Still, no one spoke openly about him because they were afraid of the Jews (Jn. 7:10-13)."

2. The Blind Man's Parents

"'We do not know how he sees now, nor do we know who opened his eyes. Ask him, he is of age; he can speak for himself.' His parents said this because they were afraid of the Jews, for the Jews had already agreed that if anyone acknowledged him as the Messiah, he would be expelled from the synagogue (Jn. 9:21-22)."

3. Joseph of Arimathea and Nicodemus

"After this, Joseph of Arimathea, secretly a disciple of Jesus for fear of the Jews, asked Pilate if he could remove the body of Jesus. And Pilate permitted it. So, he came and took his body. Nicodemus, the one who had first come to him at night, also came bringing a mixture of myrrh and aloes weighing about one hundred pounds (Jn 19:38-39)."

4. The Disciples' Fear

There are also six occasions in John's Gospel where Jesus seeks to comfort the troubled disciples with his greeting of peace as he asks them to not be afraid. The traditional Hebrew salutation was *šālôm* but Jesus' "Shalom" is a gift of salvation. His peace greeting connotes the bounty of Messianic blessing. Jesus seeks to comfort the disciples' fear in the following Gospel verses:

Jn. 6:19–20

"When they had rowed about three or four miles, they saw Jesus walking on the sea and coming near the boat, and they began to be afraid. But he said to them, 'It is I. Do not be afraid.'"

Jn. 12:15

"Jesus found an ass and sat upon it, as is written: 'Fear no more, O daughter Zion; see, your king comes, seated upon an ass's colt.' His disciples did not understand this at first, but when Jesus had been glorified, they remembered that these things were written about him and that they had done this for him."

Jn. 14:1

"Do not let your hearts be troubled. You have faith in God; have faith also in me."

Jn. 14:27

"Peace I leave with you; my peace I give to you. Not as the world gives, do I give it to you. Do not let your hearts be troubled or afraid."

Jn. 16:33

"I have told you this so that you might have peace in me. In the world you will have trouble, but take courage, I have conquered the world."

Jn. 20:19

"On the evening of that first day of the week, when the doors were locked, where the disciples were, for fear of the Jews, Jesus came and stood in their midst and said to them, 'Peace be with you.'"

LOVE AND FEAR IN 1 JOHN

In John's Epistles, the Johannine theme of love is used to support practical advice on Christian living. This theme of love is given to us as evidence in the Letters of John to show us that because God is Love, if we have the love of God and the love for one another in us, there is then no room for fear as fear will be cast out. The theme of love appears forty-six times in John's First Epistle. The love of the world and the love of God are seen to be mutually exclusive. John tells us:

> Do not love the world or the things of the world. If anyone loves the world, the love of the Father is not in him (1 Jn. 2:15).

Because of its high Christology, John's Gospel and his Letters were responsible to a great degree for the development of the Doctrine of the Trinity in the early Christian church. The Trinity would be ratified by the later church councils beginning with the Council of Nicea in 325 AD.[5] The Trinity, we are told, states that there is one God in three persons. The three are consubstantial and inseparable as they are one God. Once again, John tells us in his First Letter: "God is love (1 John 4:17)."

Love is rooted in oneness; fear is rooted in separation. In separation there is, of course, no oneness and consequently there can be no true love. Without love, fear will eventually lead us to death. Thus, in the end, there can be only love and love will lead us to eternal life (1 Jn 3:14). John will maintain that love is an opposite of fear. We find this in reading through Chapter 4 of the First Epistle of John:

> Beloved, let us love one another, because love is of God; everyone who loves is begotten by God and knows God. Whoever is without love does not know God, for God is love. In this way the love of God was revealed to us: God sent his only Son into the world so that we might have life through him. In this is love: not that we have loved God, but that he loved us and sent his Son as expiation for our sins. Beloved, if God so loved us, we also must love one another. No one has ever seen God. Yet, if we love one another, God remains in us, and his love is brought to perfection in us. This is how we know that we remain in him and he in us, that he has given us of his Spirit. Moreover, we have seen and testify that the Father sent his Son as savior of the world. Whoever acknowledges that Jesus is the Son of God, God remains in him and he in God. We have come to know and to believe in the love God has for us. God is love, and whoever remains in love remains in God and God in him. In this is love brought to perfection among us, that we have confidence on the day of judgment because as he is, so are we in this world. There is no fear in love, but perfect love drives out fear because

fear has to do with punishment, and so one who fears is not yet perfect in love (1 John 4: 7-18).

The word "love" is mentioned here twenty times in just a few short verses. Furthermore, we are told by John in 4:18 that: "There is no fear in love, but perfect love drives out fear because fear has to do with punishment, and so one who fears is not yet perfect in love (1 Jn 4:18)."

These particular verses in 1 John are the backbone of John's first letter. God's love does not punish the way human vengeance does. It disciplines and prunes to purify and perfect us to bear more fruit. The primary way Christians are to be recognized is by our love. Christian life is founded on the knowledge of God as love and on Jesus' continuing presence in the Holy Spirit that relieves us from fear of judgment. Christ gives us this confidence, even as we live and love in this world. Yet Christian love is not abstract but lived out in the concrete manner of love for one another and loving God as Christ loves us.

When we experience God's love in our lives and share it with others, there is no room for fear. Any punishment that may possibly await those who do not believe should not concern us as "abiding" believers. Only after experiencing God's love can we know with certainty that love will never die, nor will we ultimately die, but live by loving and following Christ. In following Jesus, the vertical and horizontal loving relationship we have with God and others in our lives gives us confidence and security. The ability to live out Christ's love in our lives is a sign of our faith as we follow Him.

As John tells us in his first letter, in relation to love, fear is associated with punishment. Who among us has not had an occasion where we have been immobilized by fear? Having courage, it has been said, is not the absence of fear; it is in spite of any fear. As believers in the love of Christ, we should not have an overwhelming spirit of fear if we believe that God can and will forgive us of all our sins. The one who is forgiven will then know Christ in a true loving relationship. If we love God and our neighbor, we will live for Christ and have the courage not to fear future punishment. Fear can manifest itself in many ways. Some of the many human emotional responses that might have their basis in fear are prejudice, jealousy, bias, condemnation, vengeance, discrimination, anxiety, aggressiveness, contempt, envy, doubt, and insecurity. All of these in some way work against building a loving relationship with God and others.

FEAR OF THE LORD

Finally, "Fear of the Lord" is a very different dimension of fear and is more akin to love than fear. It is fear in the sense of awe, wonder, and respect, and has its beginning in wisdom. It has more to do with reverence than actual fear in a negative sense as its basis is the love of God who first loved us. Love is a fundamental characteristic of who God is; it is God's essence and existence because as we have discussed on several occasions in this book: "God is love (1 Jn. 4:17)."

Loving God is why He created us; it is the main reason for our existence. It is primarily the work of the Holy Spirit sent by Jesus from the Father to perfect us in God's love. It is up to us to admit our fears as sometimes being the presence of sin in our lives, and we should ask the Holy Spirit to show us what is the manifestation of those fears. After that, we need only to ask for the grace of God's help to overcome all our fears through his perfect love.

NOTES

1. Ibid Ch. 4 no. 3, JBC p. 832, 80:25).
2. Brown, Raymond, ed., Jerome Biblical Commentary, (Eng. Cliffs, NJ, Prentice-Hall Publishing, 1968), Sec. 63:1–185, pp. 414–466, https://www.worldcat.org/title/new-Jerome-biblical-commentary/oclc/657161583. See also "Love, the Ultimate Reality," Michael Hickey, Get Real (Lanham, MD, Univ. Press, 2012), Ch. 6, pp. 25–26.
3. Ibid Ch. 2 no. 2.
4. Ibid Ch. 4 no. 2.
5. Kevin Knight, New Advent Catholic Encyclopedia, Source. Translated by Henry Percival. From Nicene and Post-Nicene Fathers, Second Series, Vol. 14. Edited by Philip Schaff and Henry Wace. (Buffalo, NY: Christian Literature Publishing Co., 1900.) http://www.newadvent.org/fathers/3819.htm. see also Leclercq, Henri. "Agape." The Catholic Encyclopedia. Vol. 1. (NY, New York: Robert Appleton Company, 1907). 23 Nov. 2020 http://www.newadvent.org/cathen/01200b.htm

Chapter 17

Two Extended Allegories
Parables and Allegories

There are some who refer to the stories of the Good Shepherd and the True Vine in the Gospel of John as "parables." However, this Gospel unlike the synoptic Gospels contains no parables. Even the term, "parable (*parobole*, Gk.)" appears only in Matthew, Mark, and Luke (as well as in Hebrews) about fifty times and never once in John. The Good Shepherd and The True Vine are two "allegories" or what are called (*paroimia*, Gk.) in John, which is the equivalent of a figurative discourse. They are two extended allegories and do not have any comparison in the other three Gospels. There is what could be considered as an additional third brief allegory in John, "The Grain of Wheat (Jn 12:24)." However, this is a single verse metaphor and appears to have similar refrains which are repeated in the Gospels of Matthew, Mark, and Luke (Mk.8:35, Mt. 16:25; Lk. 9:24; Mt. 10:39; Lk. 17:33). Unlike the other two which are extended allegories, this brief allegory is not particularly unique to John's Gospel.

 A parable and an allegory are different figures of speech, as a parable has the nature of a simile and an allegory has the nature of a metaphor. Then by definition, an "allegory" is a story or poem which can be understood on many levels to reveal a hidden spiritual or moral meaning. As an extended metaphor, it makes an implied comparison. As part of the allegory, abstract ideas or principles can be described in terms of certain characters, animals, figures, plants, events, or other objects to form a valuable teaching and assist in telling the story. Because the intent of an allegory in the Bible is often to convey a moral or spiritual message, the characters or objects in the allegory can typically represent virtue or vice, good or evil, truth or falsity, etc. The allegory tends toward a figurative sense as opposed to a literal interpretation as it usually has a broader enigmatic message than the words portray on the surface. A parable is a simple succinct story which illustrates a moral, ethical, instructive, or spiritual lesson. The parable often sketches a setting, describes an action, and shows the results. As an extended simile, the parable makes an expressed as opposed to an implied comparison the way an allegory does. The meaning of the parable is not intended to be hidden, as is the case with an allegory, but is mostly straightforward and often not always obvious. Some examples of familiar parables in the synoptic Gospels are the Good Samaritan (Lk. 10:25–37) and the Prodigal Son (Lk. 15:11–32).

On the other hand, some parables of Jesus did not always adhere to that last part of the definition of a parable being, "straightforward and obvious." We see this witnessed by the frequent confusion and questioning of the disciples regarding some of the parables, especially those concerning the Kingdom of God. Perhaps, the reason for this is that some of the parables, particularly those concerning the Kingdom of God, were called parables by the synoptic Gospel writers, but they were actually allegories which contained a hidden meaning. The Parable of the Sower which is found in all three synoptic Gospels is an example of a parable which is actually an allegory with a deeper message concerning the Kingdom of God (Mt. 13:1–23; Mk. 4:1–20; Lk. 8:4–15). These two extended allegories in the Gospel of John--the Good Shepard and the True Vine-contain layers and layers of hidden meaning and understanding their cryptic message can be compared to peeling off the layers of an onion.

THE GOOD SHEPHERD, JOHN 10:1–42

The Good Shepard is the first of the two extended allegories found in John's Gospel. It relates a teaching of Jesus as follows:
"Amen, amen, I say to you, whoever does not enter a sheepfold through the gate but climbs over elsewhere is a thief and a robber. But whoever enters through the gate is the shepherd of the sheep. The gatekeeper opens it for him, and the sheep hear his voice, as he calls his own sheep by name and leads them out. When he has driven out all his own, he walks ahead of them, and the sheep follow him, because they recognize his voice. But they will not follow a stranger; they will run away from him, because they do not recognize the voice of strangers. Although Jesus used this figure of speech, they did not realize what he was trying to tell them. So, Jesus said again, "Amen, amen, I say to you, I am the gate for the sheep. All who came [before me] are thieves and robbers, but the sheep did not listen to them. I Am the gate. Whoever enters through me will be saved and will come in and go out and find pasture. A thief comes only to steal and slaughter and destroy; I came so that they might have life and have it more abundantly. I am the good shepherd. A good shepherd lays down his life for the sheep. A hired man, who is not a shepherd and whose sheep are not his own, sees a wolf coming and leaves the sheep

and runs away, and the wolf catches and scatters them. This is because he works for pay and has no concern for the sheep. I am the good shepherd, and I know mine and mine know me, just as the Father knows me and I know the Father; and I will lay down my life for the sheep. I have other sheep that do not belong to this fold. These also I must lead, and they will hear my voice, and there will be one flock, one shepherd. This is why the Father loves me, because I lay down my life in order to take it up again. No one takes it from me, but I lay it down on my own. I have power to lay it down and power to take it up again. This command I have received from my Father. Again, there was a division among the Jews because of these words. Many of them said, "He is possessed and out of his mind; why listen to him?" Others said, "These are not the words of one possessed; surely a demon cannot open the eyes of the blind, can he?"

    The feast of the Dedication was then taking place in Jerusalem. it was winter. And Jesus walked about in the temple area on the Portico of Solomon So the Jews gathered around him and said to him, "How long are you going to keep us in suspense? If you are the Messiah, tell us plainly." Jesus answered them, "I told you and you do not believe. The works I do in my Father's name testify to me. But you do not believe, because you are not among my sheep. My sheep hear my voice; I know them, and they follow me. I give them eternal life, and they shall never perish. No one can take them out of my hand. My Father, who has given them to me, is greater than all, and no one can take them out of the Father's hand. The Father and I are one." The Jews again picked up rocks to stone him. Jesus answered them, "I have shown you many good works from my Father. For which of these are you trying to stone me?" The Jews answered him, "We are not stoning you for a good work but for blasphemy. You, a man, are making yourself God." Jesus answered them, "Is it not written in your law," I said, "You are gods?" If it calls them gods to whom the word of God came, and scripture cannot be set aside, can you say that the one whom the Father has consecrated and sent into the world blasphemes because I said, 'I am the Son of God'? If I do not perform my Father's works, do not believe me; but if I perform them, even if you do not believe me, believe the works, so that you may realize [and understand] that the Father is in me and I am in the Father." [Then] they tried again to arrest him; but he escaped from their power. He went back across the Jordan to the place where John first baptized, and there he remained. Many came to him and said, "John performed no sign, but everything John said about this man was true." And many there began to believe in him (Jn. 10:1-42).[1]

The allegory of the Good Shepherd is the last public teaching of Jesus which the Evangelist John will record in his Gospel. The allegory of the True Vine which will follow later in Chapter 15 is considered a private teaching as instruction for Jesus' disciples. The motif of the shepherd is used extensively throughout the books of the Old Testament (for example: Gn. 48:15; 49:24; Mi. 7:14; Ps. 23:1–4, 80:1) and particularly in the Book of Ezekiel Chapter

34:1–31. Here is found a startling prophecy which foresees the coming of a shepherd in the line of David who will one day lead the flock and a harsh critique of those false shepherds of Israel who are leading the flock astray and will be judged harshly.

Both the allegory of the Good Shepherd and the True Vine are examples drawn from nature and are consistent with the spiritual message contained in most allegories; as in the natural, so in the spiritual. In the Old Testament, the good Israelite shepherd often risked his life to protect the sheep. In this allegory, Jesus is the Good Shepherd, but Jesus is represented figuratively here not only as the Good Shepherd, but also as the gate. He has free and open entry into the sheepfold. Just as the sheep enter and leave the fold only through the gate, just so, entry is gained into God's fold only through Christ. The pasture to which Jesus is leading the sheep who hear His voice is eternal life.

This discourse will continue Jesus' earlier attacks on the Pharisees who are figuratively represented by the hired hands, strangers, thieves, and robbers in the allegory. They are reminiscent of the woeful shepherds of Israel in Ezekiel's Old Testament prophecy. They do not recognize Jesus' voice, but the sheep who are figuratively representing the people of God who follow Jesus, do recognize it. The Pharisees will then tell Jesus that he is possessed as he is "only a man who is making himself God." This will represent more of the intense irony that is prevalent in John's Gospel, for the reality is just the opposite of the accusation made by the pharisees against Jesus. What the pharisees fail to realize is that Jesus is God who has become a man.

The wolf figuratively represents the lure of this world along with sin, evil, and the temptations of the devil, which Jesus, the Good Shepherd, seeks to protect us to the point of laying down His life. The "other sheep," John has Jesus mentioning here, are perhaps a figurative reference to either the dispersed children of God or the Gentiles. The Feast of the Dedication was an event which celebrated the rededication of the altar and the re-consecration of the temple during the time of the Maccabean revolt (164 BC) after both were desecrated.[2] This may be an oblique allegorical reference to Jesus being both the new Lamb of God who will be slain at the altar and the new temple of God who is Jesus Himself. The case for this is further strengthened by Jesus' assertion a little later in the discourse that the Father has "consecrated" Him as the Son of God. Jesus' power to both "lay down His life and take it up again" is probably an implied reference to the crucifixion and resurrection which John, at the time he is writing this Gospel is viewing in the rear-view mirror. When asked by the Jewish authorities if He is the Messiah, John will have Jesus make the first open and public confession of His Sonship to them during this discourse. Previous answers to that question put to Jesus by them had been answered more ambiguously and elusively. Jesus will tell them openly now that: "He and the Father are One." Just so, the Good Shepherd will also be one with the sheep whom He calls by name. As the Holy Father Pope Francis often says: "To be a good shepherd you will have to smell like the sheep."[3]

Following Jesus' expressing His Oneness with the Father to assert the unity and power of His words and deeds, the Good Shepherd allegory will conclude with many followers who listened to Jesus' words and saw His deeds and came to believe in Him. The public ministry of Jesus which began in Chapter 1 as John the Baptist recognized Jesus as the Son of God will end here with the Good Shepard discourse. Jesus, the Son of God and the Good Shepherd, will return to the same place across the Jordan river where John was first baptizing. This was where Jesus' public ministry began and where His public ministry will end.

THE TRUE VINE, JOHN 15:1–17

The True Vine is the second of the two extended allegories found in the Gospel of John. As we saw earlier in Chapter 14 of this book, this allegory has much to say about "discipleship" and "abiding" or "remaining" in Christ:

> I am the true vine, and my Father is the vine grower. He takes away every branch in me that does not bear fruit, and every one that does he prunes so that it bears more fruit. You are already pruned because of the word that I spoke to you. Remain in me, as I remain in you. Just as a branch cannot bear fruit on its own unless it remains on the vine, so neither can you unless you remain in me. I am the vine you are the branches. Whoever remains in me and I in him will bear much fruit, because without me you can do nothing. Anyone who does not remain in me will be thrown out like a branch and wither; people will gather them and throw them into a fire, and they will be burned. If you remain in me and my words remain in you, ask for whatever you want, and it will be done for you. By this is my Father glorified, that you bear much fruit and become my disciples. As the Father loves me, so I also love you. Remain in my love. If you keep my commandments, you will remain in my love, just as I have kept my Father's commandments and remain in his love. "I have told you this so that my joy may be in you and your joy may be complete. This is my commandment: love one another as I love you. No one has greater love than this, to lay down one's life for one's friends. You are my friends if you do what I command you. I no longer call you slaves, because a slave does not know what his master is doing. I have called you friends, because I have told you everything I have heard from my Father. It was not you who chose me, but I who chose you and appointed you to go and bear fruit that will remain, so that whatever you ask the Father in my name he may give you. This I command you: love one another" (Jn 15:1-17).

The second of the two extended allegories, "The True Vine," happens to be my favorite scripture passage in the entire Bible. I will discuss more about why that is in a personal reflection immediately following the commentary on this allegory. There are numerous Old Testament passages which refer to the people of Israel as a vine: Psalm 80:8–16, Isaiah 5:1–7, Jeremiah 2:21, Ezekiel 15:1–8, 17:5–10, 19:10–14, and Hosea 10:1. "I Am the Good Shepard" and "I Am the True Vine" are two of the seven emphatic "I Am" (*Ego eimi*, Gk.) statements of Jesus in John's Gospel. As was stated in a previous chapter, the number seven to the Israelites (and to John) did historically represent perfection or completion because in the Book of Genesis, God rested on the seventh day following creation.

In this second extended allegory in John 15:1–17, Jesus will state emphatically "I Am the True Vine (Jn 15:1)." The statement by Jesus is consistent with John's High Christology and his emphasis on the divinity of Christ. The word "true" is used here in the sense of real, genuine, or authentic as opposed to the Pharisees and religious leaders who might be seen as disingenuous or inauthentic as would any wild or deformed vine. Jesus' Father is the vine grower who cultivates the vine and prunes the branches. All true disciples of Christ are the branches that will be pruned by the vine grower (the Father) to bear more fruit. The "fruit of the vine" may also be an intentional allusion to the Eucharist in John's Gospel.

Those who have fallen away from faith in Christ or who are unbelievers are the withered branches. Without remaining on the vine, they cannot bear fruit as Christ, the True Vine is the source of life for the branches. The withered branches are good for nothing more than to be thrown into the fire and burnt. This may be a figurative representation in the allegory which makes oblique reference to the eternal punishment that may await those who do not remain on the vine. The love that flows through Father and Son gives life to all branches who remain and will bear fruit in the Holy Spirit by obeying Jesus' command to "love one another (Jn. 15:17)." To live a life of Christian love it is imperative for all to remain or abide on the vine. This is so important that the word for "remain or abide" in the Greek language (*meno*, Gk.) is repeated several times in these few verses. John uses the word for "abide or remain" a total of thirty-four times in his Gospel with almost one third, or a total of twelve, repeated here in this True Vine allegory. We should also mention that the word "love" (*agape*, Gk.) is repeated nine times here. You can tell that these are both a few favorite words of the Evangelist because half of all the uses of the word *meno*, Gk. in the entire Bible are in his Gospel and the word *agape*, Gk. is used a total of fifty-seven times in his Gospel, more than the other three Gospels combined. If you will recall, both the words "abide/remain" and "love" are also two of the important sub-themes in John's Gospel which we have previously explored.

Following the two extended allegory discourses of The Good Shepard and The True Vine there appears to be much doubt and confusion on the part of the disciples as to what it was exactly that Jesus had said to them. The purpose of any allegory is to convey an enigmatic or cryptic meaning. The disciples did not appear to grasp what Jesus had been trying to tell them with these two allegorical figures of speech, and they probably did not catch the hidden meaning Jesus intended. They first conveyed their lack of understanding of figures of speech during the Good Shepard allegory (Jn. 10:6). There will be more evidence of the disciples' lack of understanding soon after as Jesus states openly that He has been speaking to them of His relationship with the Father using "figures of speech (Jn 16:25)." Furthermore, they will soon know more about that close relationship without His use of these "figures." The disciples respond to what Jesus now tells them about that relationship and His coming from the Father and soon returning to the Father by replying: "Now you are talking plainly, and not in any 'figure of speech (Jn. 16:29).'"

THE TRUE VINE, A PERSONAL REFLECTION

I don't think it would be appropriate here to talk at length about my personal experience of the True Vine, but on the other hand I would feel remiss if I didn't at least mention it briefly. Back in the early 1980's, I had left my job as a senior marketing manager in corporate America to return to school and enroll as a theology major at Weston/Boston College School of Theology and Ministry. I previously had been part of an adult Bible study program at my parish taught by a young woman by the name of Nina Lauzon Pension. She was a wonderful, spirit-filled teacher who fostered an amazing experience which opened "the eyes of my heart" to the Word of God in Scripture. Following this initial exposure to studying the Bible as the Word of God, I wanted to pursue a deeper continuous understanding of the Word in Scripture. Weston/Boston College was part of the Boston Theological Institute and the school allowed me the flexibility to work and support my family while attending the theology program to pursue a Master of Divinity studies degree.

There is an ancient Buddhist proverb which wisely promises: "When the student is ready, the teacher will come along."[4]

My faculty advisor (who also became my spiritual father and friend) was a Jesuit priest who was one of the foremost Biblical scholars in the United States, the now deceased, Fr. Daniel Harrington, SJ. Dan had authored many books on the Bible, was the editor of New Testament Abstracts for the United States, and was a contributing editor to America Magazine, the Jesuit bi-monthly. I found him to be one of the most brilliant Biblical minds I had ever met. His knowledge of the Books of the Old and New Testament was simply awe inspiring. In addition to all of that, he was one of the most humble and reverent priests I had ever met who balanced his vast Biblical knowledge with a genuine sense of humility and a delightful sense of humor.

To complete my biblical studies, I had to have some income to support my family. Upon praying and attempting to discern a direction for the necessary flexible employment, I was led to my now well-worn Bible as a starting point. I believe it was the Holy Spirit who then led me to the True Vine discourse in the Gospel of John, Chapter 15. Eventually, I came to believe that the Holy Spirit's answer for my part-time employment was wrapped up in the allegory of the True Vine in the Bible. Subsequently, I was led to find an empty storefront on a busy main street in a nearby town from where my family and I were living. From scratch, I then bought the necessary bookshelves and store furniture, ordered Christian books and Bibles, and began a Christian book store outreach. It focused on those who had either been alienated by the Christian churches such as alcoholics or divorced and separated, as well as the many Christians who voted with their feet and walked away from their church. The bookstore, on Market St., met people where they were in their Christian walk. Although I never had any intention to compete with any church, the storefront became a low-hanging branch for many to find their way back into various Christian churches and become re-attached to the vine who is Christ. The name of the Christian bookstore could only have been: "The True Vine." Although I no longer continue to operate the True Vine Bookstore. It remained open, operating, and producing fruit of the vine for another ten years after I left its day-to-day operation in other spirit-filled Christian hands.

NOTES

1. Ibid Ch.2 no. 2.
2. Kevin Knight, New Advent, McMahon, Arthur. "Feast of the Dedication (Scriptural)." The Catholic Encyclopedia. Vol. 4. (NY, New York: Robert Appleton Company, 1908).://www.newadvent.org/cathen/04673b.htm
3. Homily of Pope Francis, St. Peter's Basilica, Holy Thursday, 28 March 2013, Vatican Archives, http://www.vatican.va/content/francesco/en/homilies/2013/documents/papa-francesco_20130328_messa-crismale.html
4. Attributed to Buddha Siddhartha Guatama Shakyamuni, Ancient History Encyclopedia Online, Joshua Mark, "Siddhartha Gautama." Ancient History Encyclopedia, 23 Sep 2020. https://www.ancient.eu/Siddhartha_Gautama/

Chapter 18

Judgment and the World

JUDGMENT

The word "judge" (*mispat*, Hb., *krinos*, Gk.) means "to separate, to make a distinction between, to exercise judgment upon, to call to account, to choose judiciously, or to be brought to account." Consequently, the word "judgment" in a Judeo-Christian sense can be said to be a just and righteous opinion or decision that is based on prayerful discernment, careful thought, and reflection. The Greek root of *krinos* can mean both judgment and condemnation. God's judgment concerns the just destiny of each human soul after death. His judgment and the grace of His providence can be seen to be working hand in hand during the lifetime of every individual in the world. His judgment is always loving, just, righteous, and merciful. God's judgment is an integral part of God's nature and is characteristic of His divine prerogative. Knowing the judgments of God and how He has judged previously in scripture can give us some insights into His character. However, in this the age of the Holy Spirit, all judgment must be looked at in the light of Christ, as all judgment of the Father has now been handed over to the Son. Everyone will be judged through the lens of the Gospel of Jesus Christ who is at the center of all God's personal and universal judgments. With the crucifixion, resurrection, and ascension of Jesus Christ, all of God's judgment has now become Christocentric. There are seen to exist two of God's judgments which are coextensive—the first with the end of life on earth for the individual and the second with the end of all worldly human life at the end of time. These are often referred to as Particular Judgment and Final Judgment. It is at the Final Judgment that the eternal destiny of all creatures who have lived on earth will be decided.[1]

Throughout John's Gospel, Jesus is presented as both judging and not judging while eschatological (end times) scenarios are presented and alluded to in which humanity will be judged at the last day, and also in which there will be no final judgment for some. As the King of Siam voiced in the play, *The King and I*: "Is a puzzlement."[2] However, there does exist a hypothesis that provides a resolution to this puzzle. This resolution provides one form of judgment for those who are faith-filled Christians and believe that Jesus Christ is their Lord and Savior and another for the rest of humankind. For example, in the Gospel of John Chapter 3, John will tell us:

> For God so loved the world that he gave his only Son, so that everyone who believes in him might not perish but might have eternal life. For God did not send his Son into the world to judge the world, but that the world might be saved through Him. He who believes in Him is not judged; he who does not believe has been judged already because he has not believed in the name of the only begotten Son of God. And this is the verdict, that the light came into the world, but people preferred darkness to light because their works were evil (Jn. 3:16-19).[3]

God loved not just the world, but humankind and all life He created that exists in the world. He loves us so much that He sent his only begotten Son. As was just related, Jesus' purpose for coming into this world is not simply to judge but to save. His coming provokes judgment; some believe and are not therefore judged; others condemn themselves by not believing and turn from the light. We also learn that judgment is not only future but is partially realized in the now moment. As in the Gospel of John Chapter 5, Jesus will tell us:

> Nor does the Father judge anyone but has given all judgment to the Son. So, that all may honor the Son just as they honor the Father. Whoever does not honor the Son does not honor the Father who sent Him. Amen, amen, I say to you, whoever hears my word and believes in the one who sent me has eternal life and will not come to judgment but has passed from death to life. . .and He gave Him power to exercise judgment because He is the Son of man. Do not be amazed at this because an hour is coming in which all who are in the tombs will hear His voice and will come out, those who have done good deeds to the resurrection of life, but those who have done wicked deeds to the resurrection of judgment. I cannot do anything on my own, I judge as I hear and my judgment is just because I do not seek my own will, but the will of the one who sent me (Jn. 5:22–24, 27–30).

The Son has been given the authority to judge because He is both the Son of Man and the Son of God. Judgment can bring acquittal or condemnation. What John relates to us here is that Christian believers have been exempted from any end-time judgment process. They have already obtained the benefit of salvation and the enjoyment of eternal life in the here and now as well as the continuation of eternal life in the heavenly realm, following their earthly sojourn and subsequent death. As a contradistinction to this, there is presented here in these verses, a judgment for the rest of humanity. Christ, as God the Father's appointed judge, will sit in judgment of not only those who have rejected him outright but also those who have not had the opportunity to accept him. This hypothesis places the Johannine Christ in the position of sole judge who acts to bring eternal life to Christian believers and as the deliverer of judgment to the non-Christian portion of humanity. Here is what Jesus tells us about the judgment of the Father and that He brings not just judgment but light into the world:

> Jesus spoke to them again saying: "I am the light of the world. Whoever follows me will not walk in darkness but will have the light of life. . . . He said to them: You belong to what is below, I belong to what is above. You belong to this world, but I do not belong to this world." So, they said to him, "Who are you?" Jesus said to them, "What I told you from the beginning. I have much to say to you in judgment. But the one who sent me is true, and what I heard from him I tell the world . . . I do not seek my own glory; there is one who seeks it and He is the one who judges" (Jn. 8:12, 23, 26, 50).

And: "Jesus said, 'I came into this world for judgment, so that those who do not see might see, and those who do see might become blind (Jn. 9:39).'"

In the Nicene Creed which we repeat at Mass each week, we say the words: "He will come again in glory to judge the living and the dead."[4] This is testimony to the creedal faith we believe as our creed affirms the words of Jesus in the Gospels. The judgment that Jesus speaks of is happening right now. Just as Jesus says in John 12:31, 47–78, when people who have not accepted Christ die, they are judged by the measure they had judged by. It is not Jesus who is even necessarily judging them, it is the words He has spoken, so some are passing judgment upon themselves. With approval or condemnation, each of us exercises judgment of ourselves. We feel the result of all our unloving actions, all our lack of forgiveness, and our search for other gods such as money, status, power, and other worldly things. Many of us commit the grievous sin of putting things before people. We feel the horrendous realization that our treasure may have been laid up on earth and not heaven. Where our treasure lies, there is our God. The measure we measured by in our earthly sojourn is what is then measured back to us. On the other hand, those who love Jesus and one another and asked for forgiveness know that we are forgiven, and thus we escape the judgment that is to come because we go to Him out of love. We know that Jesus will judge us out of His love for us. He will not only forgive us but through grace will ultimately save and rescue us from judgment. Our choice will be made to either accept or refuse the grace of God that is offered us in Christ. Like all choices, there are consequences either way. Here is what Jesus tells us about principally coming to save and not to judge the world:

> Now is the time of judgment on this world; now the ruler of this world will be driven out...And if anyone hears my words and does not observe them, I do not judge him, for I did not come to judge the world but to save the world. Whoever rejects me and does not accept my words has something to judge him: the word that I spoke, it will judge him on the last day (Jn. 12:31, 47–48).

Following the crucifixion, resurrection, and ascension of Jesus Christ, He has sent the Holy Spirit from the Father who will be another advocate as Jesus was the first advocate. It will be the Holy Spirit who will then prosecute and convict the world of judgment, for Satan, the ruler of this world, will be cast out and death will be finally defeated. What will then be shown is that the basic sin was the refusal to believe in Jesus. For along with judgment, the Holy Spirit will convict the world of sin for all who have not believed in Jesus Christ and righteousness, as He ascends back to the right hand of the Father:

> But I tell you the truth, it is better for you that I go. For if I do not go, the Advocate will not come to you. But if I go, I will send him to you. And when he comes, he will convict the world in regard to sin and righteousness and judgment: sin, because they do not believe in me; righteousness, because I am going to the Father and you will no longer see me; judgment, because the ruler of this world has been judged (Jn. 16:7-11).

Finally, recall the opening words to that beautiful song:

> "Come Holy Ghost, creator blest,
> And in our heart, take up thy rest."[5]

THE WORLD

God created the "world" *(kosmos,* Gk.) as a harmonious and orderly system with spiritual as well as material realities. The root of the Greek word *kosmos* is *komeo* which means "to take care of, order, or arrange." Consequently, man's initial experience of God was first drawn from the world, i.e., creation needed a creator; an orderly system needed an orderer; an arrangement needed an arranger; the persons (and things) of the world who were taken care of needed a caretaker. John has Jesus speaking at great length about the world, particularly as it relates to Jesus Himself and to judgment. In fact, of the one hundred eighty-eight times that the word "world" appears in the New

Testament of the Bible, one hundred four of these are in the Gospel and letters of John the Evangelist. At times the word *kosmos* or "world" may refer to either the entire universe, all of creation, or this planet and its inhabitants. Whenever Old Testament writers wanted to draw a distinction between the world and the universe, they would often say, "The heavens and the earth (Gn. 1:1)" or similar words drawn from these to describe the universe. Oftentimes, the people of the world are simply referred to as "the world," and even occasionally "world" can refer to those who do not accept Jesus as Lord or even those who hate Him (Jn. 7:7) or hate his followers (Jn. 15:18–19). The word itself must depend on the frame of its reference and how it is being used at any one time in order to comprehend its intended meaning.

In 1986, while attending Weston School of Theology (now part of The Boston College School of Theology and Ministry), I was blessed to be able to cross register into a few courses being taught at Harvard Divinity School by the late theologian and spiritual author, Fr. Henri Nouwen. I had the unique opportunity to not only study under him, but along with my wife, Terri, to socialize and dine with him in a few off-campus settings. One of Fr. Nouwen's most oft-repeated phrases both in and out of class was: "Whatever is most personal is most universal and whatever is most universal is most personal."[6]

When we pray for even one person, the matter becomes universal. It is reminiscent of an ancient Spanish proverb which states: "Cada persona es un mundo," which translated means: "Each person is a world."[7] Therefore, in His providence, God cares for every person as if they were an entire world.

God's judgment encompasses the world as we know it. In Noah's time, God judged the world as He flooded the earth, and at the end of time, the Parousia, the Second Coming of Christ, He will judge the world and its inhabitants. In the meantime, we are somewhere in between, as every day the world is the evidence of God's love and care for his creatures as well as the locus of His judgment activity. Because God created the world and humankind, the world has a history which God set in motion at the beginning. The world's history reached its high point with the incarnation, crucifixion, and resurrection of Jesus Christ along with the outpouring of the Holy Spirit. Following this, the world has now currently entered its eschatological (i.e end times) phase where the outcome of the world's history is already decided by Christ. This outcome remains hidden from our eyes and can only be seen through the eyes of faith along with hope and love.

Meanwhile, as John's Gospel will illustrate, there are powers at work in the world which are hostile to God and the transformation of the world in Christ. In John's Gospel and his letters, "world" (*kosmos*, Gk.) most often refers to the people of the world and not the planet or the universe. Even more particularly, "world" as John understands the word and conveys its usage to us, can be defined as "everything that is opposed to God." We know this is the case because otherwise Jesus would not call Satan, "the ruler of this world whom Jesus will cast out (Jn. 12:31-33; 14:30; 16:11)." The first time John the Evangelist mentions "the world" is at the Gospel's opening, in the *Logos* Prologue of Chapter 1. He tells us almost from the start that even though the world came to be through Him, the world did not know the *Logos*: "The true light which enlightens everyone was coming into the world. He was in the world and the world came to be through Him, but the world did not know Him (Jn. 1:9-10)."

Soon after the *Logos* Prologue, John will tell us through John the Baptist that Jesus, the Lamb of God, was sent into the world to take away its sins. *The Agnus Dei*, The Lamb of God, is thought to have derived its title from the paschal lamb, whose blood saved Israel in the ancient world. The story of the paschal lamb is found first in the Old Testament Book of Exodus, Chapter 12:1–28. The root of the title could also partly reflect the suffering servant who was led like a lamb to the slaughter as a sin-offering. This was prophesied by Isaiah in Is. 53:7–10. John the Evangelist would later write in the Book of Revelation, Chapters 5, 6, and 7 as well as in 17:14, about the victorious apocalyptic lamb who would take away the sin of the world as John the Baptist prophesied and would destroy evil in the world: "The next day (John the Baptist) saw Jesus coming toward him and said, 'Behold, the Lamb of God, who takes away the sin of the world (Jn. 1:29).'"

The Lamb of God was sent into the world to save and not to judge it; to take away the sin of the world. When we comprehend how undeserving the world and its people are of God's love then we can understand how great a gift that God has given us in His Son. Jesus had told us that He came into the world not to judge the world, but to save it and that those who believe in Him are not judged:

> For God so loved the world that he gave his only Son, so that everyone who believes in him might not perish but might have eternal life. For God did not send his Son into the world to judge the world, but that the world might be saved through Him. He who believes in Him is not judged; he who does not believe has been judged already because he has not believed in the name of the only begotten Son of God. And this is the verdict, that the light came into the world, but people preferred darkness to light because their works were evil (Jn. 3:16-19).

John will confirm this for us again further on as well through the woman at the well and the Samaritan townspeople. Here we are told that we are called to believe in the saving power of Jesus Christ because Jesus, the Son of God, is truly the Savior of the world: "and they said to the woman, 'We no longer believe because of your word; for we have heard for ourselves, and we know that this is truly the Savior of the world (Jn. 4:42).'"

After the fourth sign in John's Gospel, The Multiplication of the Loaves, Jesus is first seen as the Prophet, like Moses or Elijah, who has come into the world. In the Discourse on the Bread of Life, He will soon let them know that He is much more than this. Jesus is the Bread of Life who has come into the world to bring life to a world that has hungered, not simply for bread to ease their hunger, but for the spiritual bread of eternal life which is in Him. Consequently, because eternal life is in Him, He is the life of the world. There is strong evidence here of a world transforming Eucharistic theme[8] that John is trying to bring out:

> When the people saw the sign He had done, they said, "This is truly the Prophet, the one who is to come into the world. . . . For the bread of God is that which comes down from heaven and gives life to the world. . . . I Am the living bread which came down from heaven; whoever eats this bread will live forever; and the bread that I will give is my flesh for the life of the world (Jn. 6:14, 33, 51).

After the religious leaders taunt Jesus, they ask Him to declare that he is the Son of God publicly, and to manifest Himself to the world. Soon after He will tell His followers that it is the world which hates Him because He exposes many who manifest the world's evil: "No one works in secret if he wants to be known publicly. If you do these things, manifest yourself to the world...The world cannot hate you, but it hates me, because I testify to it that its works are evil (Jn. 7:4, 7)."

Jesus declares Himself to be "The light of the world" so that those who follow Him will not walk in darkness but will have the light of life. He does not belong to this world, He belongs to the Father's world above. The religious leaders belong to this world and it is His words that will judge them. Jesus relates that what the Father has told Him is what He has come to tell the world:

> Jesus spoke to them again saying: "I am the light of the world. Whoever follows me will not walk in darkness but will have the light of life. . . . He said to them: You belong to what is below, I belong to what is above. You belong to this world, but I do not belong to this world." So, they said to him, "Who are you?" Jesus said to them, "What I told you from the beginning. I have much to say to you in judgment. But the one who sent me is true, and what I heard from him I tell the world" (Jn. 8:12, 23, 26, 50).

He makes the claim again in Jn. 9:5 that He is the Light of the world as He heals the man who was born blind from birth. He will explain metaphorically in Jn 9:39 that He has come into the world that the blind might see. Light is needed to see. So, Jesus in declaring Himself to be the "Light of the world" is bringing forth the spiritual connotation of this statement. He will also bring out the reverse as the reason He has also come into the world, i.e., "to make the seeing blind (the Pharisees)." The beggar moves from first seeing Jesus as a man (Jn. 9:11), to then seeing him as a prophet (Jn.9: 17), to worshiping him as Lord (Jn.9:38). The Pharisees move in the opposite direction. They say: "This man [Jesus] is not from God (Jn. 9:22)." Then they threaten the people of the synagogue with: "If anyone should confess Jesus to be the Messiah, he will be put out of the synagogue (Jn. 9:24)." They then tell the man born blind from birth: "This man [Jesus] is a sinner (Jn. 9:34)." What will ultimately become clear in the last three verses is that what began as a miracle of healing physical blindness has become a miracle of healing spiritual blindness for the blind man and the opposite for the religious leaders. They think that they see but are in effect, spiritually blind. Even though He has come into the world as its Savior, there are some in the world who will say, "we see," but will be judged as John relates: "While I am in the world, I am the light of the world. . . . Then Jesus said, 'I came into this world for judgment, so that those who do not see might see, and those who do see might become blind (Jn. 9:5, 39).'"

Soon after declaring Himself to be the "Light of the World," Jesus attends the Feast of the Dedication which is an eight-day festival of lights (*Hanukkah*, Hb.).⁹ This feast celebrates the Maccabees' rededication of the altar and re-consecration of the temple in 164 B.C. (see 1 Mc 4:36–59; 2 Mc 1:18–2:19; 10:1–8). In addition to being the world's light, Jesus will also draw a metaphorical comparison to His being "consecrated" by the Father as well as being the new temple of God and newly rededicated altar as Son of God sent into the world: "Can you say that the one whom the Father has consecrated and sent into the world blasphemes because I said, 'I am the Son of God (Jn. 10:36)?'"

And soon after, as Jesus comes out to Bethany to raise Lazarus from the dead, He will declare Himself once more to be the "Light of the World." It will be Martha this time who will use a summary of titles that were brought out earlier in John's Gospel. She will testify that Jesus is indeed Lord and Messiah, the Son of God who has come into the world as its Savior. Jesus says to Martha: "Are there not twelve hours in a day? If one walks during the day, he does not stumble, because he sees the light of the world. . . . Martha said to him, 'Yes, Lord. I have come to believe that you are the Messiah, the Son of God, the one who is coming into the world (Jn.11:9, 27).'"

Jesus has just shown the crowd the seventh sign in raising Lazarus from the dead. To the Pharisees, who see the crowd following after Jesus, it appears that now the whole world is chasing after Jesus. John, however, is using the word "world" as another use of showing irony. Here the word is intending to show the universality of salvation and its use is similar to how John used it in the scene of the woman at the well and the Samaritan townspeople. At this time, they all declare: "Truly this was the Savior of the world (Jn. 4:42)."

Jesus will soon tell all who are listening that you must hate your life in this world in order to keep it unto eternal life: "So, the Pharisees said to one another, 'You see that you are gaining nothing. Look, the whole world has gone after him. . . . Whoever loves his life loses it, and whoever hates his life in this world will preserve it for eternal life (Jn. 12:19, 25).'"

Jesus has come as Savior of the world, but Satan has been the ruler of this world. Judgment is upon him and he is about to be cast out as Jesus leaves this world to return to the Father in the world above. The Holy Spirit, the Spirit of Truth, is about to be sent into this world by Jesus from the Father. The Holy Spirit will use the words of Jesus to pass judgment upon all those in the world who have rejected Jesus and not accepted His words: "Now is the time of judgment on this world; now the ruler of this world will be driven out...And if anyone hears my words and does not observe them, I do not judge him, for I did not come to judge the world but to save the world. Whoever rejects me and does not accept my words has something to judge him: the word that I spoke, it will judge him on the last day (Jn. 12:31, 47-48)."

In Chapter 13 we are told that Jesus knew that His hour had come to pass from this world to the Father. Furthermore, that He loved his own in the world and he loved them to the end (Jn. 13:1). Jesus will be sending the Holy Spirit, (another advocate because Jesus was the first advocate) when He departs from this world. He already knows that the world will not accept the Holy Spirit because it is "the Spirit of truth" which the world doesn't know. Although Jesus is leaving, he will be leaving His disciples His peace which the world cannot give. Jesus' *shalom* is a gift of salvation; it is a Messianic blessing.

As Jesus departs and the Holy Spirit comes to indwell believers as Jesus' new way of being present in the world, Satan, evil, and death will be cast out of the world. Here is what Jesus tells us:

> the Spirit of truth, which the world cannot accept, because it neither sees nor knows it. But you know it, because it remains with you, and will be in you. I will not leave you orphans; I will come to you. In a little while the world will no longer see me, but you will see me, because I live and you will live. . . . Judas, not the Iscariot, said to him, "Master, [then] what happened that you will reveal yourself to us and not to the world? . . . Peace I leave with you; my peace I give to you. Not as the world gives, do I give it to you. Do not let your hearts be troubled or afraid . . . I will no longer speak much with you, for the ruler of the world is coming. He has no power over me, but the world must know that I love the Father and that I do just as the Father has commanded me. Get up, let us go (Jn. 14:17-19, 22, 27, 30-31).

Jesus came into this world from the Father and prepared Himself to leave this world and return to the Father in the world above. First, He will tell His disciples that if the world hates them, so be it; the world hated Him first. Any peace His followers will experience is in Jesus because all that they will get from the world is a heap of trouble. Therefore, they must take courage and remember that Jesus has conquered the world: "Amen, amen, I say to you, you will weep and mourn, while the world rejoices; you will grieve, but your grief will become joy. . . . I came from the Father and have come into the world. Now I am leaving the world and going back to the Father. . .I have told you this so that you might have peace in me. In the world you will have trouble, but take courage, I have conquered the world (Jn. 15:18; 16:20, 28, 33)."

Jesus' glory was preexistent, He shared it with the Father before the world began. Now through Jesus' coming hour of crucifixion, resurrection, and ascension (seen as one event in John's Gospel), He will return all glory to the Father as the Father glorifies Him. Because the world can include people who hate Jesus and His followers, He prays for His disciples and asks the Father to protect them while they are still in the world. In fact, Chapter 17 in its entirety is called "The High Priestly Prayer" of Jesus. It is a prayer of petition for all of Jesus' immediate as well as His future disciples. As Jesus was sent into the world by the Father whom the world does not know, He had commissioned the disciples and sent them into the world as well. Although Jesus is still in the world, while reciting this prayer, He is viewing His mission to this world as a thing of the past (Jn. 17:4, 11–12). Jesus will ask the Father for the oneness of unification so that He and the disciples will be one with the Father—the Father and Jesus in them and they in the Father along with Jesus. This will be a perfect oneness of mutual love to show the world. Jesus begins His prayer by asking the Father to glorify Him:

> Now glorify me, Father, with you, with the glory that I had with you before the world began. . . I pray for them. I do not pray for the world but for the ones you have given me, because they are yours, And now I will no longer be in the world, but they are in the world, while I am coming to you. Holy Father, keep them in your name that you have given me, so that they may be one just as we are. . . As you sent me into the world, so I sent them into the world. so that they may all be one, as you, Father, are in me and I in you, that they also may be in us, that the world may believe that you sent me. I in them and you in me, that they may be brought to perfection as one, that the world may know that you sent me, and that you loved them even as you loved me. (Jn. 17:4–5, 9–12, 18, 21–23).

Jesus will answer Pilate that His Kingdom: "is not of this world (Jn. 18:36)." Pilate who maintains that he should not be judging Jesus according to Jewish law is now taken aback by Jesus' response because "kingship" could now be seen as a political crime and not simply a religious question for the Jews to handle on their own. Jesus has been born into this world to save rather than judge, but also to testify to the truth. Pilate does not see that the Truth is standing right in front of him as he asks: "What is truth (Jn. 18:38)?"

After Jesus' departure from this world, the Holy Spirit will be coming into this world in a new way. The Holy Spirit who is the Spirit of Truth will then testify to the truth and testify that Jesus is The Truth. All who belong to the truth will listen to Jesus' voice, both as recorded here in the Gospel but also as spoken through the Holy Spirit. Unlike the Gnostic heresies[10] which John the Evangelist is addressing in part through his Gospel, The Gospel of Jesus Christ contains no secret knowledge as Jesus has spoken publicly to the world. This is reaffirmed as Jesus answers Pilate:

> Jesus answered him, "I have spoken publicly to the world. I have always taught in a synagogue or in the temple area where all the Jews gather, and in secret I have said nothing. . . . At this, Pilate said to them, "Take him yourselves, and judge him according to your law." The Jews answered him, "We do not have the right to execute anyone." Jesus answered, "My kingdom does not belong to this world. If my kingdom did belong to this world, my attendants [would] be fighting to keep me from being handed over to the Jews. But as it is, my kingdom is not here." So, Pilate said to him, "Then you are a king?" Jesus answered, "You say I am a king. For this I was born and for this I came into the world, to testify to the truth. Everyone who belongs to the truth listens to my voice" (Jn. 18:20, 31, 36–37).

As was said earlier, the Epilogue (Chapter 21) is seen as a second epilogue and a later addition by a disciple of John. The chapter was added, however, before written copies were made and this Gospel was widely disseminated. The Epilogue appears in all of the earliest manuscripts uncovered. The redactor will bring John's Gospel to its universally accepted and its canonical conclusion by stating that there wouldn't be enough books in the whole world that could contain the things that Jesus did which are not recorded in this Gospel:

> There are also many other things that Jesus did, but if these were to be described individually, I do not think the whole world would contain the books that would be written (Jn. 21:25).

NOTES

1. McHugh, John. "Particular Judgment." The Catholic Encyclopedia. Vol. 8. New York: Robert Appleton Company, 1910. 24 Nov. 2020 http://www.newadvent.org/cathen/08550a.htm. MLA citation. McHugh, John. "General Judgment." The Catholic Encyclopedia. Vol. 8. New York: Robert Appleton Company, 1910. 24 Nov. 2020, http://www.newadvent.org/cathen/08552a.htm

2. Rodgers, Richard, 1902–1979. Rodgers And Hammerstein Present a Musical Play: The King and I. [Place of publication not identified]: Milwaukee, WI, Williamson Music Co.; Exclusively distributed by Hal Leonard, 1951.

3. Ibid Ch. 2 no. 2.

4. Wilhelm, Joseph. "The Nicene Creed." The Catholic Encyclopedia. Vol. 11. New York: Robert Appleton Company, 1911. 24 Nov. 2020 http://www.newadvent.org/cathen/11049a.htm

5. "Come Holy Spirit", Rabanus Morris, author, Catholic Book of Worship #416, https://hymnary.org/hymn/CBOW1994/416

6. "Personal/Universal," Henri Nouwen, Reaching Out, (NY, NY, Penguin/Random House, 1986).

7. Meditation, Magnificat, (Yonkers, NY, November 2020), Vol. 22, no. 9, www.magnificat.com

8. Ibid Ch. 4 no.3, Brown, Raymond, ed., Jerome Catholic Encyclopedia. Vol. 4. (NY, New York: Robert Appleton Company, 1908). 24 Nov. 2020 http://www.newadvent.org/cathen/04673b.htm

9. Arendzen, John. "Gnosticism." The Catholic Encyclopedia. Vol. 6. (NY, New York: Robert Appleton Company, 1909). 24 Nov. 2020 http://www.newadvent.org/cathen/06592a.htm. Biblical Commentary, (Englewood Cliffs, NJ, Prentice-Hall, 1968), 63:24; 80; 49–51, pp. 414–466, 837.

10. McMahon, Arthur. "Feast of the Dedication (Scriptural)." The Catholic Encyclopedia. Vol. 4. (NY, New York: Robert Appleton Company, 1908). 24 Nov. 2020 http://www.newadvent.org/cathen/04673b.htm

11. Arendzen, John. "Gnosticism." The Catholic Encyclopedia. Vol. 6. (NY, New York: Robert Appleton Company, 1909). 24 Nov. 2020 http://www.newadvent.org/cathen/06592a.htm

Chapter 19

Son of Man-Son of God

SON OF MAN

At the end of the first chapter of John following the *Logos* Prologue, Jesus will be found among the first disciples who are each asked by another disciple in turn to "come and see." John will first use the title "Son of Man" in a revelation by Jesus to Nathanael as one of the first disciples: "And he said to him, 'Amen, amen, I say to you, you will see the sky opened and the angels of God ascending and descending on the Son of Man (Jn. 1:51).'"[1]

Son of Man was the primary title Jesus used throughout all four Gospels to describe or refer to Himself. But what do you think the title "Son of man" meant to John and to Jesus? Jesus refers to Himself eighty times in all four Gospels as "Son of Man" and ten times in John's Gospel.

In a dialogue with Nicodemus, as He did with Nathanael, Jesus will again use the title twice more referring to His ascending and descending from heaven and being born from above. Furthermore, listen closely to John's words in the third chapter of his Gospel as he refers to Jesus as both "Son of Man" and "Son of God," while in the same passage he speaks about ascent and descent in relation to Jesus. Here is what he says:

> "No one has ascended to heaven except the one who has descended from heaven, the Son of Man. And just as Moses lifted up the serpent in the desert, so must the Son of Man be lifted up, so that everyone who believes in him may have eternal life." For God so loved the world that he gave his only Son, so that everyone who believes in him might not perish but might have eternal life. For God did not send his Son into the world to condemn the world, but that the world might be saved through him. Whoever believes in him will not be condemned, but whoever does not believe has already been condemned, because he has not believed in the name of the only Son of God (Jn. 3:13-18).

This will soon be followed by Jesus' declaring to all who were following Him and listening, that as the "Son of Man" He has descended from heaven, being sent on a mission to mankind by the Father. There are several references to the "Son of Man" also being the "Son of God" here as well. Jesus will go as far as to declare that He and God the Father are one, with His having been given the power to receive honor, to give the Spirit and eternal life to all who believe in Him, and to judge. This will infuriate the Jews and especially many of the religious leaders who will soon seek to kill Him (Jn. 5:19–27; 6:27; 6:53–62).

As God the Father's Ambassador, Jesus has come into the world as its light. There will be several references to the Son of Man being "lifted up." This can be seen on many prophetic levels including Jesus later being glorified while lifted up on the cross, Jesus rising and being lifted up from the dead, and finally, Jesus lifted up from the earth and ascending back to the Father in heaven:

> So must the Son of Man be lifted up. . . . So Jesus said (to them), "When you lift up the Son of Man, then you will realize that I AM, and that I do nothing on my own, but I say only what the Father taught me. . . . So the crowd answered him, "We have heard from the law that the Messiah remains forever. Then how can you say that the Son of Man must be lifted up? Who is this Son of Man?" (Jn. 3:14; 8:28; 12:34)

Ordinarily, "Son of Man" could be just an oblique way of referring to your own self with special reference to your human fragility and frailty. Just as the title "Son of God" could sometimes refer to Jesus' divinity, "Son of Man" could sometimes refer to Jesus' humanity, but it's not all as simple as that. There is more to it. In the Old Testament, the prophet Ezekiel used the title "Son of Man" more than Jesus did in the Gospels, ninety-four times in fact. There are some similarities to the manner in which Jesus used the title in Matthew, Mark, and Luke. The title in Ezekiel is used more as a common idiom to express that it is a human being and distinct from the divine. However, the use of this title by Jesus in John's Gospel is very different than what is implied by Ezekiel or what it often implies in the synoptic Gospels. Rather than use the "Son of Man" title the way Ezekiel did, John seems to use the title more in line with the reference to it in the Old Testament Book of Daniel. In Daniel, worldly kingdoms are typically represented by grotesque beasts, but the coming of the eternal Kingdom of God is represented by the "Son of Man" who receives dominion, power, worship, and Kingship. In Chapter 7:13–14 Daniel writes:

> As the visions during the night continued, I saw coming with the clouds of heaven One like a "Son of Man." When he reached the Ancient of Days and was presented before him, He received dominion, splendor, and kingship; all nations, peoples and tongues will serve him. His dominion is an everlasting

dominion that shall not pass away, his kingship, one that shall not be destroyed (Dn. 7:13-14).

John will reaffirm this intended usage and implications of the title "Son of Man," not only in his Gospel but in the Book of Revelation which he authored after his Gospel was written (see Rv. 1:13, 14:14). In the Book of Revelation, here is what John writes:

And in the midst of the lampstands (stood) one like a Son of Man, wearing an ankle-length robe, with a gold sash around his chest (Rv. 1:13).

Then I looked and there was a white cloud and sitting on the cloud one who looked like a Son of Man, with a gold crown on his head and a sharp sickle in his hand (Rv. 14:14).

The title "Son of Man" which Jesus uses to refer to Himself in John's Gospel describes one who is more a kind of human intermediary figure, a God-Man, a transformed human, both who descended from the world above and is ascending back to the Father. In John's Gospel, He is the *Logos* figure who first descends from heaven to become the point of contact between heaven and earth. He brings with Him, heavenly glory, power and authority, the ability to destroy evil, offer eternal life, judge men, and establish God's reign on earth. "Son of Man" when used by Jesus to refer to Himself in John's Gospel doesn't just refer to His humanity as we know it, just as being God's Son and the second person of the Trinity is more than being a son of God. We are told in Luke's Gospel that even Adam could claim to be a son of God (Lk. 3:38).

Just so, when Jesus refers to Himself as "Son of Man," He is saying more than I am a son of humankind. As "Son of Man," John is describing Jesus as the actual communication of divine life (Jn. 6:53) bringing new birth from above, descending to earth and subsequently imparting this new birth to believers through His Spirit when he ascends again.

"Son of Man," as the principal title used by Jesus in the Gospel of John, describes His intimate relationship between being Jesus of Nazareth who descended from heaven in human flesh to be born of Mary by the Holy Spirit and the eternal personal relationship with God the Father He had from the beginning. The title also describes the saving-relationship He has with us and all those who believe in Him throughout all time on earth. We see an example of this depicted by John as Jesus restores the sight of the man who was born blind and subsequently comes to believe in Jesus as the Son of Man and worships Him: "Do you believe in the Son of Man?" He answered and said, "Who is he, sir, that I may believe in him?" Jesus said to him, "You have seen him and the one speaking with you is he." He said, "I do believe, Lord," and he worshiped him (Jn. 9:35).

Unlike the synoptics, John will portray Jesus death on the cross continuously as the beginning of the Son of Man's hour of glorification as well as the Father's glorification in and through Jesus:

> The hour has come for the Son of Man to be glorified . . . Jesus said, "Now is the Son of Man glorified, and God is glorified in him. If God is glorified in him,] God will also glorify him in himself, and he will glorify him at once" (Jn. 12:23; 13:31-32).

Finally, in the Old Testament, Israel is often spoken of as a vineyard or as a vine. We find this to be the case in several books of the Old Testament (for example, Isaiah 5:1–7, Psalm 80:9–18, Sirach 24:17, Jeremiah 2:21, Ezekiel 15:2; 17: 5–10; 19:10, and Hosea 10:1). The identification of the vine with the Son of Man is particularly evident in Psalm 80:15–18, as the nation of Israel prays that one day a Davidic king will eventually lead them as this victorious Son of Man:

> Turn back again, God of hosts; look down from heaven and see; Visit this vine, the stock your right hand has planted, and the son whom you made strong for yourself. Those who would burn or cut it down—may they perish at your rebuke. May your hand be with the man on your right, with the Son of Man whom you made strong for yourself (Ps. 80:15–18).

This Old Testament Psalm is referenced and carried forward in The Parable of the True Vine as John metaphorically shows a close identification of Jesus, the Son of Man, with the vine as well (Jn. 15:1–17). As we are told in this parable, the life we receive only bears fruit if we remain as a branch on the vine who is Jesus.[2]

SON OF GOD

Following the *Logos* Prologue in Chapter 1, John the Baptist is the first to bear witness that Jesus is the Son of God. His testimony is based on having seen the Spirit of God descend from the sky like a dove and remain on Jesus. Seeing this, he believes is a sign from God that reveals to him that Jesus will be the one who will baptize with the Holy Spirit and is therefore, the Son of God. Here is what the Baptist says:

> I saw the Spirit come down like a dove from the sky and remain upon him. I did not know him, but the one who sent me to baptize with water told me, "On

whomever you see the Spirit come down and remain, he is the one who will baptize with the Holy Spirit." Now I have seen and testified that he is the Son of God (Jn. 1:33-34).

Almost immediately following the Baptist's witness, one of Jesus first disciples, Nathanael, will bear witness as well: "Nathanael answered him, 'Rabbi, you are the Son of God; you are the King of Israel (Jn. 1:49).'"

The designated title "Son of God" had been often used in the Old Testament as a title of adoption for the Davidic king (2 Sm. 7:14; Ps. 2:7, 89:27). The title used here by Nathanael along with "King of Israel" also brings out Nathanael's seeming recognition that Jesus is the Messiah. For the Gospel writer John, "Son of God" and "King of Israel" will necessarily indicate Jesus' divinity. As discussed in the previous section above, the titles "Son of Man" and "Son of God" will sometimes be used simultaneously as they were in Jesus' dialogue with Nicodemus in Chapter 3 and when Jesus speaks to the Jews and the religious officials in Chapter 5. This would also be the first time the words "eternal life" will be used by the evangelist. This will highlight the salvific role that is intrinsic to Jesus' mission from the Father and the main reason that the Father sent the Son of God into the world. Anyone who believes in Jesus will find salvation and be offered the gift of eternal life. Those who do not believe in the name of the only Son of God will condemn themselves for their unbelief. The eternal life Jesus speaks of is in Him just as it was in the Father and he can give it to whomever He wishes. All power to exercise judgment has also been handed over to the Son of God from the Father as well (Jn. 3:13–18; 5:19–27).

In this Gospel, Jesus makes claims such as, "Before Abraham was, I AM (Jn 8:58)"; also "I and the Father are one (Jn 10:30)" and "If you've seen me, you've seen the Father (Jn. 14:9)." These are all statements of Jesus you find only in the Gospel of John and that is striking because in Matthew, Mark, and Luke as well as the writings of Paul, there is no indication that Jesus said such things. You would think that the synoptic Gospel writers and the Apostle Paul would have mentioned that Jesus called Himself "Son of God" if that was what he was declaring about Himself. However, we find this to be the case only in John's Gospel. One of the reasons this may be the case is that the Evangelist John is writing at a much later time than the other Gospel writers. He is writing his Gospel at a time when many heretics have arisen in the Christian community. They are questioning the divinity of Jesus which John believes must be defended emphatically. In John, as Jesus makes the above claims and declares His oneness with the Father, the Jews will seek to stone and kill Him for making what they believe is the claim to be the Son of God. As a man, Jesus is making Himself one with God. To the

Jews, especially the religious leaders, what they are seeing and hearing is completely blasphemous:

> "The Father and I are one." The Jews again picked up rocks to stone Him. Jesus answered them, "I have shown you many good works from my Father. For which of these are you trying to stone me?" The Jews answered him, "We are not stoning you for a good work but for blasphemy. You, a man, are making yourself God." Jesus answered them, "Is it not written in your law, 'I said, "You are gods"'? If it calls them gods to whom the word of God came, and scripture cannot be set aside, can you say that the one whom the Father has consecrated and sent into the world blasphemes because I said, "I am the Son of God?" (Jn. 10:30-36).

In the raising of Jesus' friend Lazarus from the dead, He will display the kind of power that only God can possess. Jesus will see this act of raising the dead to life as a means for the Son of God to glorify the Father and the Son. After telling Martha that He is the "Resurrection and the Life" and anyone who believes in Him will not die but live, He will ask her if she believes this. She will then bear witness to Him and give testimony that she does believe that He is both the Messiah and the Son of God:

> When Jesus heard this he said, "This illness is not to end in death, but is for the glory of God, that the Son of God might be glorified through it . . . Jesus told her, "I am the resurrection and the life; whoever believes in me, even if he dies, will live, and everyone who lives and believes in me will never die. Do you believe this?" She said to Him, "Yes, Lord. I have come to believe that you are the Messiah, the Son of God, the one who is coming into the world." (Jn. 11:4, 25-27)

The Holy Spirit will be the continuing presence of the Son of God on earth once Jesus returns to the Father. Just prior to Jesus telling the disciples about sending the Paraclete following His departure, Jesus will reiterate that the glory of the Father is evidenced through the works of the Son. This is because the Son of God is in the Father and the Father is in the Son. For this reason, we may ask anything in the name of Jesus. He tells us:

> Whatever you ask in my name, I will do, so that the Father may be glorified in the Son. If you ask anything of me in my name, I will do it. (Jn. 14:13-14).

Several times, Jesus had openly testified to His oneness with the Father in the presence of the Jewish religious leaders (see for example Jn. 5:18–25; 6:37–42; 8:35–40, 53–59; and 10:30–36). In these afore-mentioned verses, John will make it known that they are seeking to kill Jesus for what they see as blasphemy. Toward the conclusion of John's Gospel at the trial before Pilate, the Jewish religious leaders along with the crowd will cry out for Jesus to be crucified. Ultimately, they will cite their law as the primary reason why Jesus must die. The title "Son of God" was as much of a problem for the Jews from a religious perspective, as the title "King of the Jews" was for Pilate from a political perspective because it could indicate rebellion from Rome. Here are the reasons given by the Jewish religious leaders and for Pilate's ultimate willingness for condemning Jesus and sending Him to the cross:

> The Jews answered, "We have a law, and according to that law he ought to die, because he made himself the Son of God...Consequently, Pilate tried to release him; but the Jews cried out, "If you release him, you are not a friend of Caesar. Everyone who makes himself a king opposes Caesar." (Jn. 19:7, 12)

At the very conclusion of John's Gospel in the original epilogue, John himself in his final words to us will bear witness to Jesus being the Son of God.[3] He will also cite his primary reason for writing this Gospel in a purposeful summation:

> Now Jesus did many other signs in the presence of [his] disciples that are not written in this book. But these are written that you may [come to] believe that Jesus is the Messiah, the Son of God, and that through this belief you may have life in his name (Jn. 20:30-31).

NOTES

1. Ibid Ch. 2 no. 2.

2. Ibid Ch. 4 no.3, (a) Brown, Raymond, ed., Jerome Biblical Commentary, (Englewood Cliffs, NJ, Prentice-Hall, 1968), "Son of Man", Sec. 43: 113, 164, 169; 44:60–64, 88–130; 61:14, 63:57–85; 78:28–52, also pp. 414–466. (b) See also "Son of Man," McBrien, Richard, ed., Catholicism, (NY, NY, Harper-Collins Publishing., 1966), pp. 431–433, 519–520. (c) See also "Jesus Christ," Rahner, Karl SJ, ed., Encyclopedia of Theology, Seabury Press, NY, NY, 1975, pp 730–772.

3. Ibid Ch. 19 no. 2, "Son of God", (a) Sec. 42:31, 70; 43:9, 60, 113; 44:34, 53, 83, 166; 45:52, 68; 53:16; 61:9–12, 16–38. See also (b) pp. 431–433, (c) pp. 730–772.

Chapter 20

Spirit, Paraclete, and Truth

WHAT IS TRUTH?

Let's talk first about the theme of "truth" in John's Gospel because it can be somewhat confusing. John will use the words "true" or "truth" in the Greek *aletheia* and *alethes*, forty-nine times in his Gospel. For example, Pilate will ask the question: "What is truth (Jn. 18:38)?" [1]

His question alone indicates that "truth" to Pilate is something abstract. Pilate is really searching for what the late-night talk show host Stephen Colbert describes as "truthiness."[2] Indeed, Pilate was searching for some kind of "truthiness" but not "truth," and certainly not "The Truth" who was standing there right in front of him. As regards Truth, John will have Jesus issuing one of the seven "I AM" emphatic statements in his Gospel: "I AM the Way, the Truth, and the Life (Jn. 14:6)."

To John, Jesus is the "Truth" in person. Jesus who is the Son of God is also God's very Truth. Later, John will have Jesus saying in the same chapter that The Paraclete who is to come will be: "The Spirit of Truth (Jn. 14:16)."

The prediction of Jesus' hour of glorification as coming and his later sending of the Spirit was predicted by him earlier in John, Chapter 4:23–24. In speaking to the woman at the well, Jesus will tell her that all this must occur so that true worshippers might worship the Father who is Spirit in "Spirit and Truth." Jesus tells her:

> But the hour is coming, and is now here, when true worshipers will worship the Father in Spirit and truth; and indeed, the Father seeks such people to worship him. God is Spirit, and those who worship him must worship in Spirit and truth (Jn. 4:23-24).

To Jesus, the "Truth" will also be the Holy Spirit who will be coming into the world when Jesus departs and sends the Paraclete who is "The Spirit of Truth." When John uses the words "true" or "truth," he most often does not mean "true" as opposed to "false." His intention is more to convey someone or something "real" or "veritable" (which is from the Latin word "*veritas*," meaning "truth"). When Jesus says: "I AM the Way, the Truth and the Life" (Jn. 14:6) or "I AM the True Vine" (Jn. 15:1) or when John says: "Jesus is the true light" (Jn. 1:9) or the "true bread" (Jn. 6:32), John is conveying a synonym or metaphor for "real" or "veritable." His threading of "true" and "truth" thematic statements throughout his Gospel has the underlying intention of conveying that Jesus Christ is the revelation of "ultimate reality."[3]

Right from the beginning of his Gospel in the Prologue, John will start to describe Jesus this way when he uses the term *the Logos*, the Word, attempting to convey to Christian believers, both then in the Christian community as well as believers throughout all time, that Jesus is essentially Ultimate Reality. Moreover, it will be the Paraclete, "the Holy Spirit," "the Spirit of Truth," who will not only testify that Jesus is the "Truth," but will also guide us as followers of Jesus to all "the truth." John will have Jesus tell us:

> But when he comes, the Spirit of Truth, he will guide you to all truth (Jn. 16:13).

SPIRIT AND PARACLETE

Let's talk now about the words, "spirit" and "paraclete" as an intricate part of this theme in John's Gospel. Immediately following the *Logos* Prologue in Chapter 1, we find John the Baptist giving testimony to Jesus that he would be the one on whom God's Spirit came down like a dove and remained, and although John baptized with water, it would be Jesus who would baptize with the Holy Spirit. Here is the testimony given by the Baptist:

> John testified further, saying, "I saw the Spirit come down like a dove from the sky and remain upon him. I did not know him, but the one who sent me to baptize with water told me, 'On whomever you see the Spirit come down and remain, he is the one who will baptize with the holy Spirit'" (Jn. 1:32–33).

A little later Jesus will tell Nicodemus that no one can enter the Kingdom of God unless they are born from above, being "born of water and Spirit (Jn 3:5-8)." From the earliest periods of Israel's history, the spirit was known as the dynamic power of God, as well as the word and wisdom of God, revealing and conveying God's word and life to God's people. The spirit had always been the instrument of God's self-revelation throughout the Old Testament. For the Israelites, the spirit of the Lord bore a close likeness to the wisdom of God. As it had been stated previously in the Book of Wisdom for example: "The spirit of the Lord fills the whole world (Wi. 1:7)."

One of the things that I always had found confusing was this: If the Spirit of God was always and ever in the world and filled the world since the beginning of time, then how is it that the Holy Spirit was sent by Jesus after that? Well, the difference is that with the death and resurrection of Jesus, the Holy Spirit of God came into the world in a brand new way. This could only happen after the Spirit was made new with the death and resurrection of Jesus. Once the glorification of Jesus had occurred, the living water, the newness of Jesus' life in the Spirit was sent into the world and given to believers. Here is what the Gospel writer John tells us that would verify that:

> He who believes in me as the scripture has said, "Out of his heart shall flow rivers of living water." Now this He said about the Spirit, which those who believed in Him were to receive; for as yet, the Spirit had not been given, because Jesus was not yet glorified. (Jn. 7:38-39).

The word, "spirit" is not often used in John's Gospel, especially as compared to the synoptic Gospels and in particular, Luke's Gospel. "Paraclete," is John's unique designation for the Holy Spirit. It is a term used exclusively by John and is not found in any of the other Gospels or anywhere in the Apostle Paul's letters or anywhere else in the entire Bible for that matter. And it should be noted here that the Paraclete is, "another Paraclete," because Jesus was the first Paraclete. This we are told in John, Chapter 14:

> If you love me, you will keep my commandments. And I will ask the Father, and he will give you another Advocate to be with you always, the Spirit of truth, which the world cannot accept, because it neither sees nor knows it. But you know it, because it remains with you, and will be in you. I will not leave you orphans; I will come to you. (Jn. 14:15-18)

The English word "Paraclete" comes from the Greek *Parakaleo* and it has several different nuanced meanings depending on John's usage of the word. It literally means in the Greek, "called to one's side." The primary meaning renders it as an "advocate," but it can also mean "comforter," or "helper," or "counselor." It is best to determine the specific meaning dependent on John's usage of the word in any particular verse.[4] This is due to the fact that John brings the Paraclete into his Gospel suddenly and without any specific introduction. In the days of early television broadcasts, it would be somewhat comparable to the manner in which variety show host Ed Sullivan used to introduce Elvis Presley or the Beatles[5]: "And now, needing no introduction, the Paraclete…"

Overall, the best way for us to picture the Paraclete is as our defense attorney. John will tell us that the Paraclete is sent by the Father through Jesus. We often talk about the procession of the Holy Spirit from the Father through the Son whenever we recite the Nicene Creed (*Nicene-Constantinople Creed*)[6].

This sub-theme in which John includes the Paraclete will thread primarily through three continuous chapters of his Gospel, Chapters 14, 15, and 16. Let's look at some of those verses on the Paraclete in those three chapters:

> "If you love me, you will keep my commandments. And, I will ask the Father, and he will give you another Advocate to be with you always, the Spirit of truth, which the world cannot accept, because it neither sees nor knows it. But you know it, because it remains with you, and will be in you. I will not leave you orphans; I will come to you. In a little while the world will no longer see me, but you will see me, because I live and you will live. On that day you will realize that I am in my Father and you are in me and I in you. Whoever has my commandments and observes them is the one who loves me. And whoever loves me will be loved by my Father, and I will love him and reveal myself to him." Judas, not the Iscariot, said to him, "Master, [then] what happened that you will reveal yourself to us and not to the world?" Jesus answered and said to him, "Whoever loves me will keep my word, and my Father will love him, and we will come to him and make our dwelling with him. Whoever does not love me does not keep my words; yet the word you hear is not mine but that of the Father who sent me. 'I have told you this while I am with you. The Advocate, the Holy Spirit that the Father will send in my name—he will teach you everything and remind you of all that [I] told you (Jn. 14:15-26).'"

And: "When the Advocate comes whom I will send you from the Father, the Spirit of truth that proceeds from the Father, he will testify to me. And you also testify, because you have been with me from the beginning (Jn. 15:26–27)."

And also:

> But I tell you the truth, it is better for you that I go. For if I do not go, the Advocate will not come to you. But if I go, I will send him to you. And when he comes he will convict the world in regard to sin and righteousness and condemnation: sin, because they do not believe in me; righteousness, because I am going to the Father and you will no longer see me; condemnation, because the ruler of this world has been condemned. "I have much more to tell you, but you cannot bear it now. But when he comes, the Spirit of truth, he will guide you to all truth. He will not speak on his own, but he will speak what he hears, and will declare to you the things that are coming. He will glorify me, because he will take from what is mine and declare it to you (Jn. 16:7-14)."

The Paraclete, the Holy Spirit, will be the divine presence of Jesus who will be coming again at the Parousia (the Second Coming).[7] In the meantime, "between the acts" so to speak, the Father will not be leaving us defenseless as we were told by Jesus in John's Gospel: "I AM coming back to you (Jn. 14:3)."

We see that the activity of the Paraclete will begin with Jesus' return to the Father. The coming of the Paraclete will also involve the coming of the Son and the Father. In much the same way as Jesus was glorified in the Father, the Paraclete will glorify both the Father and the Son. The Paraclete will be revealing the mind of Christ (Jn. 16:13) as Christ revealed the mind of the Father (Jn. 14:10). The current age, the church age, will be the age of the Holy Spirit to whom will be attributed the divine presence of the Father and the Son in mystical and sanctifying grace and in public testimony. For now, the Paraclete will be sent both to followers of Christ and to an unbelieving world throughout the life of the church which is the deposit of the Holy Spirit. As we heard, in Jn. 15:17, 26–27 and in Jn. 16:13, the Paraclete is called "the Spirit of Truth" and will be guiding the church into all truth. The Paraclete will reside in the church and will remain or abide in every Christian believer. This began right after Jesus' glorification through His crucifixion and resurrection and as soon as He appeared to his disciples, breathed on them, and said: "Receive the Holy Spirit (Jn. 20:22)."

The role of the Paraclete is highlighted by John in the passages we just read and the Paraclete's role will be multivariant. As we reflect on those verses, we can see the multi-faceted role the Paraclete will be given:

Roles of the Paraclete, Chapters 14, 15, and 16

1. The Paraclete will be a "COMFORTER" to us as the continuing presence of Jesus.
2. The Paraclete will be a "COUNSELOR" and "TEACHER" after Jesus is gone.
3. The Paraclete will be a "WITNESS" to give testimony to Jesus and the Father, to us as believers, and also to an unbelieving world.
4. The Paraclete will be an "ADVOCATE" and along with Jesus will be a "MEDIATOR" on our behalf before God in the heavenly court.
5. The Paraclete will be a "JUDGE" convicting the world of sin and righteousness and judgment.
6. The Paraclete will not only be a "REVEALER" of the truth, but moreover, will be a GUIDE to all truth. And finally:
7. The Paraclete will "EMPOWER" us as a community of believers to worship God in spirit and truth.

Let me end our discussion on the Paraclete with a short story as related to me by one of my first Bible study teachers to make a final point here about the Holy Spirit sent by Jesus Christ. I have always liked stories, don't you like stories?

The Story of the Little Child in the Crib

As momma lay her little child down and put her in the crib for the night, she kissed her tenderly and said: "You can go to sleep now precious because Jesus is right here in your room with you."

The child lay down and a few minutes later, the little girl stood up in the crib, crying and yelling for her momma. The mother came back into the room and said once again: "Go to sleep; I told you, Jesus is right here in the room with you."

The child lay down again and in less than a minute later was screaming and hollering at the top of her lungs for her momma. The mother came back into the room once more, and this time the little child stood up in the crib and said to her momma: "Mommy, I know Jesus is right here in the room with me but stay here with me for a little while because I just need someone with a little skin on them right now."

NOTES

1. Ibid Ch. 2 no. 2.
2. "Truthiness", Colbert, Stephen, The Colbert Report, Comedy Partners, Oct.,2005, http://www.cc.com/video-clips/63ite2/the-colbert-report-the-word————truthiness
3. Ibid Ch.4 no. 3.
4. "Paraclete," Harper, Douglas, Etymology Online Dictionary, Nov. 2020, https://www.etymonline.com/search?q=paraclete
5. "The Beatles," The Ed Sullivan Show, (NY, NY, CBS Broadcasting, Feb. 1964), https://www.youtube.com/watch?v=JC0MEF6d1eU
6. Kevin Knight, New Advent, Wilhelm, Joseph. "The Nicene Creed." The Catholic Encyclopedia. Vol. 11. (NY, New York: Robert Appleton Company, 1911). 26 Nov. 2020 http://www.newadvent.org/cathen/11049a.htm
7. Ibid Ch. 6 no. 5.
8. Attribution, Nina Lauzon Pension, Word of God Catholic Bible Study, (Lynnfield, MA, Our Lady of the Assumption Church, 1980).

Index

abiding and discipleship, 3, 10, 107–112, 141–143
Adonai, 65
Adoptionism heresy, 9
"Against Heresies," 9
agape (love), 57–58, 123–135
Agnus Dei. *See* Lamb of God
allegories, 137–144
Alpha and Omega, 8, 100
Apostles' Creed, 97
Apostolic Age, 57–58
apostolic witnesses, 90–91
Aquinas, Thomas, 109, 120
Aristotle, 18
ascension of Jesus, 2, 7, 97–98, 148
ascent and descent, 3, 10, 93–98, 157–158
Athanasian Creed, 26
Augustine, 4, 52, 102

background to John's Gospel, 5–14
Baptism, 117–120
Battle Hymn of the Republic, 52
Beatitudes, 7
believing, 69–74
beloved disciple, 5,59, 125, 129–130
blindness, 32, 39–41, 87–91, 118–119, 131, 151–152
blood, 119–120

Boethius, 101–102
Book of Glory, 2, 6, 10, 47–53
Book of Job, 21–22
Book of Proverbs, 21–22
Book of Revelation, 7–8, 24–25, 27–28, 93
Book of Signs, 2, 6, 10, 29–45, 113–121
Book of Sirach, 21–22
Book of Wisdom, 14, 21–22, 166
born again, 94–95
Boston College School of Theology and Ministry, 149
bread and water, 3, 11, 113–121
Bread of Life, 36–38, 66, 95, 113–116, 151
brotherly–sisterly love (phileo), 123–135
Brown, Fr. Raymond, S. J., 12, 87

Cana wedding, 32–33
Catholic Biblical Association, 12
Cerinthus, 79
Chalcedon, Council of, 26
Christological heresies, 8–9
Christology, from below, above, high, low, 7, 25–26, 93
church councils, 9, 58
church Fathers, 5, 9,
Circle of Life, 100, 105

Cloud of Unknowing, 75
Constantine, Emp, 26
Council of Trent, 120–121
cross of Christ, 29–30, 126–129
crucifixion of Jesus, 2, 47–53, 119–121, 126–129, 148

darkness. *See* light and darkness
dating of John's Gospel, 6
D'Elbee, Fr. Jean, 24
death, 99–105
Dei Verbum, Dogmatic Constitution, Vat II, 12
descent and ascent. *See* ascent and descent
destiny, 145
discipleship, 107–112, 141
Divine Wisdom, 21–22
divinity of Christ, 9–10
Divino Afflante Spirito encyclical, 12
Docetism heresy, 9
doxa/doxology, 48
dualism in John, 11, 79–80, 81–86, 87–91, 93–98

early Christian theologians, 26
Ego Eimi. *See* "I AM"
El Greco, 5
El Shaddai, 63–64
elements of a story, 1
Elohim, 63–64
Ephesus, 6–7
Epilogue, 2, 7, 10, 13, 55–59, 129, 155, 163
eros(love), 123
essence of God, 63–67, 102
eternal life, 3–4, 6, 10, 44–45, 95–97, 99–105, 116, 146–147, 153, 159
eternity and time, 99–105
ethical teachings, 7
Eucharist, 29–30, 36–38, 113–116, 151
evangelizing, 123–124
experiential knowledge, 76–77
extended allegories, 137–144

Faith and Believing, 3, 10, 69–74
"faithing," 73
Father (God), 63–67, 71–72, 95–97, 99–105, 107–112, 125–128, 142–143, 145–156, 157–163, 165–170
fear (and love), 130–135
fear of the Lord, 135
Feast of the Dedication,152
feeding of the 5000, 36–38
figures of speech, 143
following Jesus. *See* discipleship
Fruit of the Spirit, 76, 112

glory, Book of Glory, glorification of Jesus, 2, 6, 10, 47–53, 85, 160
Gnostics, Gnosticism heresy, 8–9, 79–80
God. *See* Father; Jesus Christ; Holy Spirit
Golden Thread of Augustine, 52
good and evil, 85,93
Good Samaritan, 138
Good Shepherd, 6, 66, 93, 124, 138–141
Grain of Wheat, 137

Hanukkah, 152
Harrington, Rev. Daniel J.,S.J., 139–140Healey, Mary (scripture scholar), 8
healing of the blind man, 39–41
healing of the royal official's son, 34
healing the paralyzed man, 35–36, 118
healings, 34–41, 118
Hellenism, 8,
Heraclitus, 18
heresy, 8–9, 57–58, 79–81
heresies, Arian and Nestorian, 26
High Priestly Prayer of Jesus, 50–52, 154
Historical–Critical Bible study method, 12–14, 55
Holy Spirit, 3, 67, 72–73, 76–78, 85, 94–97, 103, 107–112, 118, 124–129, 145–156, 157–163, 165–170

"I AM" Sayings, 3, 10, 12, 63–67, 70–71, 165–166
I AM Who I AM(YHWH), 63–67
Ignatius of Antioch, 5–6
Irenaeus, 5, 9, 79

Jacob's ladder, 94
Jehovah (God), 65
Jehovah Witnesses and John, 23
Jerome Biblical Commentary, 12, 120, 122
Jesus Christ, 2, 7–12, 20–28, 31–45, 47–52, 63–67, 69–73, 76–78, 83–85, 90–91, 93–97, 99–103, 107–112, 113–121, 123–135, 138–144, 145–156, 157–163, 165–170
Jesus as the *Logos*, 17–28
John the Baptist, 82, 110–112, 150, 160–161, 166
John 3:16, 123–124
Joseph of Arimathea, 89, 131–132
judge, 145
judgement, Particular and Final, 145
Judgment and the World, 3, 11, 145–156

kābôd, 48
King of Siam (*King and I*), 145–146
King of the Jews, 154–155, 163
Kingdom of God, 3–4, 6, 44, 97, 99–100, 158
knowing and loving (K. Rahner), 75
knowing and unknowing, 3, 10, 75–80
knowing God, 75–79

Lamb of God (Agnus Dei), 24–25, 150
last supper, 6
Lazarus, 7, 41–45, 125, 152, 162
life and death, 3, 10, 99–105
light and darkness, 3, 10, 81–86
light as a metaphor, 83–85
Light of the World, 66, 81–86, 151–152
lion-like lamb, 24–25, 150
little child's bedtime story, 170
loaves and fishes, 36–38

Logos and *Logos* Prologue, 2, 9–10, 14, 17–28, 81–82, 100, 110, 150, 157, 160, 166
Lord's Prayer, 7
love and fear, 45, 130–135
love and obedience, 126–130
love one another, 6, 10, 123–135

Maccabean Revolt, 140, 152
Martha of Bethany, 6, 125, 152
Martyr, Justin, 79
martyrdom, 111
Mary, Mother of God, 5, 128–129
Mary Magdalene, 6, 96–97, 128
Messiah, 2, 70, 90, 115–116, 131, 140, 152
metaphors in John, 83–85, 137
miracle, 29–31
misunderstandings of Jesus, 11–12
multiple meanings in John, 11
multiplication of the loaves, 36–38, 113, 151

Nathaniel, 89, 94, 157, 161
Nestorianism heresy, 9
New Age, 80
Nicean Council and Creed, 26, 133, 147, 167–168
Nicodemus, 7, 89, 93–95, 131–132, 157, 161, 166
Nouwen, Rev. Henri, 149

obedience (and love), 126–130

Parable of the Sower, 138
parables and allegories, 137–144
Paraclete, 7, 10, 108–109, 145–156, 165–170; roles of, 169
Passover, 6
Patmos, 7–8
Pelagianism heresy, 9
Pension, Nina Lauzon, 143, 170f
perceptual knowledge, 77
personal and universal, 149

Peter the apostle, 6, 57–59, 103, 115, 129–130
Philo, 18–19
Plato, 18
Polycarp, 5, 79
Pool of Bethesda, 35–36
Pope Francis, 141
Pope Pius XII, 12
Prado Collection, 5
Prodigal Son, 138
Prologue. *See Logos* and *Logos* Prologue

Rahner, Karl, 75
raising of Lazarus, 41–45
real presence, 116
realized eschatology, 44
remain (abide), 70, 108–112, 141–143
resurrection and the life, 44, 66, 99–105, 162
resurrection of Jesus, 2, 51–52, 66, 96–97, 115–121, 148
"The Rose"(Bette Midler), 104–105
Rubens, Peter Paul, 5

sacrament, 29–32, 115
Satan, 150, 153
Savior of the world, 151–153
seeing and blindness, 3, 10, 39–41, 81–86, 87–91
Sermon on the Mount, 6
seven (the number), 30–32
seven signs. *See* Book of Signs
Shekinah Glory, 47–48, 52
sign, 29–45, 99, 115
Son of God, 3, 10, 94, 146, 150–152, 157–163
Son of Man, 3, 10, 95–96, 116, 146, 157–163
Spirit, Paraclete, and Truth, 3, 10, 165–170
spiritual blindness, 39–41, 81–86, 87–91, 151–152
spiritual knowledge, 77
spirituality in John, 11

Stoics, 18
Sublime Exchange, 24
subordinate symbols, 82
sub–themes 3, 10–11
suffering servant (Isaiah), 48, 150
symbol, 29–31, 115
symbolism in John, 11, 29–31, 81–86, 87–91, 115
synoptic Gospels, 3–4, 6–7, 127

Tertullian, 79
theme, 1–4, 10–11
theological anthropology (of Karl Rahner), 75
Thomas the apostle, 7, 56, 72, 91, 97
time, timelessness. *See* eternity and time
transcendence of God, 102
the transfiguration, 6
the Trinity, 26–28, 128, 133, 159
True Vine, 6, 66, 108–109, 141–144, 160
True Vine Bookstore, 143–144
truth, 66, 70, 154–155, 165–170
"truthiness," 165
two allegories, 10–11, 137–144

unbelief, unbelieving, 70
universe, 149

Vatican Council II, 12, 27
vertical vs. horizontal Gospels, 93–94
Vine of Israel, 66, 160

walking on water, 39
washing of the feet, 6, 119
water, 117–121
water into wine, 32–33
the Way, 66
the Way, the Truth and the Life, 66, 69
wedding at Cana, 2, 32–33
wisdom: Old Testament (*hokmah*), 22, 166; personification of, 22, 166
wisdom of Hellenism (*sophia*), 22
woman at the well, 7, 117–118, 150–151
woman caught in adultery, 7, 95–96

women in John's Gospel, 6–7
wonder, 29–31
the Word. *See Logos* and
　Logos Prologue

works of Jesus, 29–31, 99
world. *See* Judgment and the World

Yahweh (YHWH), 63–67

About the Author

Michael Hickey is a graduate of Northeastern University., Boston, MA, and a Master of Divinity Studies' graduate of Weston Jesuit/ the Boston College School of Theology and Ministry, Boston, MA. Following a career as a corporate executive for a Fortune 500 company, he became a Director of two 501 C-3 charitable nonprofits. He has had four books previously published; *Get Goodness, Get Real, Get to the End*, and *Catholic Social Teaching and Distributism*. The books were published by University Press of America and Hamilton Books/Rowman & Littlefield Publishing Co., Lanham, MD. Michael Hickey is married to Theresa, who is a published poet and the editor of all his books. In their fifty-plus years of marriage they have raised four happy and "well adjusted" children into adulthood and they have seven grandchildren.

www.ingramcontent.com/pod-product-compliance
Lightning Source LLC
Chambersburg PA
CBHW061349300426
44116CB00011B/2053